ZEN FILMMAKING 2

Further Writings on the Cinematic Arts

SCOTT SHAW

Buddha Rose Publications

Zen Filmmaking 2:
Further Writings on the Cinematic Arts
Copyright © 2016 by Scott Shaw
www.scottshaw.com
ALL RIGHTS RESERVED

This book contains material protected under International and Federal Copyright Laws and Treaties. Any unauthorized reprint or use of this material is prohibited. No part of this book may be reproduced or transmitted in any form or by any means, electronic or mechanical, including photocopying, recording, or by any information storage and retrieval system without express written permission from the author or the publishing Company.

Rear cover photograph of Scott Shaw
by Hae Won Shin
Copyright © 2016 All Rights Reserved.

First Edition 2016

ISBN 10: 1-877792-88-8
ISBN 13: 9781877792885

Library of Congress Control Number: 2016930120

Printed in the United States of America

10 9 8 7 6 5 4 3 2 1

ZEN FILMMAKING 2
Further Writings on the Cinematic Arts

Contents

Foreword   7
Introduction   9

Section I: The Philosophy   15
Zen Filmmaking: The Definition   17
Zen Filmmaking: The Manifesto   20
Zen Filmmaking:
    Understanding the Cinematic Art   32
Zen Filmmaking
    and the Philosophy of Filmmaking   40
Zen Filmmaking X 2 or 3   42
Zen Filmmaking: Process Verse Product   44
Zen Filmmaking and What is a Zen Film   48
Zen Filmmaking: Now and Zen   53
Zen Filmmaking & the Non-Narrative Film   56

Section II: Question & Correspondence   59
Q&A   61
Zen Filmmaking:
    The Process in a Nutshell   62
Questions and Correspondence   64
Talkin' Collaboration   86
Film Scoring   89
Talkin' Distribution   90

Section III: The Technique(s)   93
Acting for the Camera   95
Working with the Actor   98
Understanding Improv Acting   101
Filmmaking Verse Video Making   105
DSLR Cinematography   108
Filmmaking and Urban Realism   111
Do Something Every Day   113

Section IV: The Zen Films   **115**
Would You Ever Do
    Another Roller Blade Seven?   **117**
What Happened to the Sword?   **120**
Legend of the Roller Blade Seven   **122**
Max Hell Frog Warrior: The Evolution   **127**

Section V: Inside Hollywood   **133**
Hollywood's Just a State of Mind   **135**
Hollywood: The Impossible Game   **138**
Film Reviews: Fact or Fiction   **141**
Getting it Right, Getting it Wrong   **144**
imdb.com: Fact or Fiction   **149**
Everybody Wants to Do Something
    But Nobody Does Anything   **153**
You Weren't There So You Don't Know   **156**
Too Famous for All the Wrong Reasons   **158**
Understanding the Influences   **162**
Terminator 2   **166**
The Only Bad Movies I'm In Are My Own   **172**
Want To Be in a Movie?   **174**
Is That Who You Are?   **178**
When You Believe   **181**
Nobody Remembers Their Name   **184**
End of an Era   **187**
Saying Everything That I Said   **192**
The Scott Shaw Guide to Must See Cinema   **195**
The Rules of Filmmaking

Section VI: Asked and Answered   **199**
Inside Zen Filmmaking   **201**
Speaking with the Zen Film Master   **211**

Scott Shaw Books-in-Print   **231**

Forward

Zen Filmmaking was never designed to be a formalized or structured process of film creation whereby a filmmaker must follow a precise set of rules and guidelines. In fact, it is just the opposite. Zen Filmmaking was devised to provide a method to make the filmmaking process as natural, as free, and as unhindered as possible. Meaning, Zen Filmmaking is about leaving behind as many obstacles and constrains from the filmmaking process as possible and emerging with a piece of cinematic art.

In Zen Filmmaking there are no rules and no definitions. There is no one way to make a Zen Film. As such, no two Zen Filmmakers will ever use the exact same set of techniques in their process of film creation. This being stated, there are certain techniques, designated in the Zen Filmmaking ideology, that can help to make the filmmaking process easier and more enlightening.

In my previous writings on filmmaking; most notably in the books: Zen Filmmaking and Independent Filmmaking: Secrets of the Craft I have attempted to provide the reader with some techniques and some personal experiences that may allow them to create the film of their dreams in the most stress-free process possible while sidestepping many of the known hindrances. In this book it will be no different. Presented will be recent writings; discussing filmmaking practices, philosophies, realizations, and descriptions of interactive personal experiences with people and/or filmmaking situations that will hopefully provide the reader with a new and unique understanding in order to make the filmmaking process not simply a road to film creation but a true pathway to cinematic enlightenment.

Introduction

Here is a thesis on Zen Filmmaking that was published to the internet several years ago, composed by an anonymous author. In a nutshell, it defines the philosophy and ideology of Zen Filmmaking about as precisely as anyone could. As such, it is provided here as an introduction to the cinematic art of Zen Filmmaking.

Scott Shaw and Zen Filmmaking

Zen Filmmaking is a unique style of film creation that was designed, developed, and propagated by Scott Shaw, with assistance from Donald G. Jackson, beginning in 1991. Aside from Shaw and Jackson, since its inception numerous filmmakers have come to embrace this spiritually inspired and free flowing style of filmmaking, including such notable directors as Sofia Coppola, Gus Van Sant, and Steven Soderberg.

Defining Zen Filmmaking

Zen Filmmaking is a formalized style of filmmaking that was developed in 1991 by Scott Shaw in association with Donald G. Jackson. The primary premise behind *Zen Filmmaking* is that no screenplay should be used in the creation of a film.

According to Scott Shaw, "In *Zen Filmmaking*, the spontaneous creative energy of the filmmaker is the only defining factor. This allows for a spiritually pure source of immediate inspiration to be the only guide in the filmmaking *process."* Donald G. Jackson stated, *"The basis of Zen Filmmaking is Spontaneous Creativity. We don't use scripts because this would limit the instantaneous nature of Zen Filmmaking. This does not mean that Zen Filmmaking is chaotic improve. It is not! What occurs is that Dr. Shaw and I study our cast and location like an empty canvas that we want to create a painting upon. We sense the energy and then move forward guiding the actors to say the right things and do the right actions – which ultimately construct a form of cinematic art."*

In his book on the subject, Shaw details there are six tenets that lay the foundation for *Zen Filmmaking.*

The Six Tenets of Zen Filmmaking:
1. Make all unpredicted situations work to your advantage.

2. Don't waste time, money, and energy attempting to create your sets when you don't have to. Instead, travel to them and allow their natural aesthetics to become a part of your film.

3. Just do it. 99% of the time you can get away with it.

4. Never let your storyline dominate your artistic vision. Too many would be filmmakers attempt to write what they believe is a *"Good"* script and then try to film it. Without an unlimited budget it is virtually impossible to get what is on the page upon the stage.

5. Zen Filmmaking is a spontaneous process. Just as the Zen understanding of enlightenment teaches that though you may meditate for years it is not until the moment when you step beyond your thinking mind and realize that you are already enlightened that you achieve *Satori.* Thus, if you acutely plan your productions, with screenplays, storyboards, and locations, there is no room for the instantaneousness of filmmaking enlightenment to occur and you will always be lost between the way your mind desired the scene to be and the way it actually turns out.

6. Ultimately, in *Zen Filmmaking* nothing is desired and, thus, all outcomes are perfect.

Labeling

A unique element of *Zen Filmmaking,* which helps to define a particular film as a, Zen Film, can be witnessed in its onscreen labeling. Whereas a traditional film most commonly begins with the statement, *"A Film By,"* a film made in the style of *Zen Filmmaking* begins with the words, *"A Zen Film By."* There is also a unique closing associated with *Zen Filmmaking.* The final credit for most traditional films reads, *"The End."* In *Zen Filmmaking*, however, the final credit is, *"The Zen."*

Comparison and Contrast

Zen Filmmaking is often compared to *Direct Cinema* or *Cinéma Vérité.* This comparison is primarily based upon the fact that all of these styles of filmmaking employ the use of improvisational acting and are filmed with

11

techniques similar to those used in the creation of a documentary film. Similar to both *Direct Cinema* and *Cinéma Vérité*, *Zen Filmmaking* relies heavily upon the edit of the film to create the final product. This is because as there are no screenplays used in the creation of these films, the edit is what is ultimately used to define the story and present what the audience will view. Shaw states, however, *"Many people have written, and I am told that it is taught in a few university courses on filmmaking, that Zen Filmmaking is the next step in the evolution of Cinéma Vérité and Direct Cinema. This is not the case, however. When Donald G. Jackson and I made the first Zen Films we did not base our ideologies upon any previously defined style of filmmaking. It was a completely organic process."*

The first film created in this style of filmmaking was the 1991 feature *The Roller Blade Seven*. In this film, such well-known actors as two-time Golden Globe winner and Academy Award nominee Karen Black appear, as do Clint Eastwood co-stars Don Stroud and William Smith.

Since its initial inception, Shaw has gone on to create numerous features in this style of filmmaking, as did Jackson until his passing from Leukemia in 2003. In addition, a number of other filmmakers have come to embrace *Zen Filmmaking* and created their own Zen Films due to its ease of cinematic creation. Filmmakers in the United States, India, Finland, Austria, and Indonesia have each embraced *Zen Filmmaking*.

Whereas some filmmakers have chosen to employee *Zen Filmmaking* as a filmmaking technique, other have used it as a source for parody. In 2007 filmmakers at Grand Valley State University in Michigan created an extended mockumentary on Scott Shaw and the making of a Zen Film.

Subdivisions

There are two noticeable subdivisions within *Zen Filmmaking*. The first is the *Zen Speed Flick*. A *Zen Speed Flick* is defined as, "A feature length film that has been cut down to its most essential elements, leaving only the most interesting and fast pasted moments." Shaw has re-cut several of his Zen Films, including: *Max Hell Frog Warrior, Guns of El Chupacabra,* and *Samurai Vampire Bikers from Hell,* thereby creating *Zen Speed Flicks* from their original content.

The second noticeable subdivision is the, *Zen Documentary*. This style of film is based on the same spontaneous creation precepts as *Zen Filmmaking*, but instead of presenting a fictional storyline, this style of Zen Film presents a documentary based presentation. Examples of Zen Documentaries are: *Dinner and Drinks, Frogtown News, Interview,* and *Imelda*.

Books and Articles

Scott Shaw has written a number of articles on the subject of *Zen Filmmaking*. He states that these articles are designed to help filmmakers remove as many obstacles as possible from the filmmaking process. Shaw has also written a book on the subject entitled, *Zen Filmmaking*.

Prior to his passing, Donald G. Jackson also wrote on the subject of *Zen Filmmaking* via his website. In addition, both filmmakers have been interviewed extensively on the subject. Articles about the filmmakers and *Zen Filmmaking* have appeared in magazines across the globe. Most recently articles and interviews on Scott Shaw and his *Zen Filmmaking* process have appeared in the United States, Japan, Hong Kong, and Azerbaijan.

Zen Films:

To date, there have been over three hundred feature films and documentaries based in the *Zen Filmmaking* style of creation.

SECTION I:
Zen Filmmaking: The Philosophy

Zen Filmmaking: The Definition

When I first coined the term, *Zen Filmmaking*, during the period when Donald G. Jackson and I were making, *The Roller Blade Seven*, it was simply a means to categorize and loosely define what we were doing – based upon our metaphysical perception of reality and filmmaking. Give it a name for those who were working with us and wondered what we were doing. I never assumed that over two-decades later there would still be a need to be clarifying the subject. That being said, when people saw *The Roller Blade Seven* that was when the discussion of *Zen Filmmaking* truly began…

Don was very big on interacting on the Internet prior to his passing in 2003. That kind of stuff never interested me. He would go around the various chat rooms and newsgroups that were up at the time and, in many cases, get into on-line confrontations with people about what and how we were doing what we were doing. In those chat rooms he discussed *Zen Filmmaking*, which really set its concept into Internet motion.

After RB7 and with the creation of films such as *Samurai Vampire Bikers from Hell, Samurai Johnny Frankenstein, Samurai Ballet, Max Hell Frog Warrior, Ride with the Devil, Guns of El Chupacabra, The Rock n' Roll Cops,* and my writings on the subject being published, people then began to further form their own opinions about *Zen Filmmaking*. The word spread… Some wrote that what we were doing was *Direct Cinema* or *Cinema Verite.'* But, that wasn't the case. We were doing what we were doing, based upon nothing done before. It was completely organic.

As the discussion continued, some filmmakers begin to move forward, using elements of the *Zen Filmmaking* philosophy, and they began to make their own Zen Films. All good...

As Don's health faded and I moved forward with Zen Films such as *Hollywood P.D. Undercover, Undercover X, Hitman City, Super Hero Central,* and *Vampire Blvd.* the word of *Zen Filmmaking* spread further. And it has continued to spread. People have continued their discussion about *Zen Filmmaking*. It is written about in several books, numerous articles, detailed in courses at a number of universities, and even a few documentaries have been made on the subject. All this being the case, the reason I was, (in some-ways), forced to formally define *Zen Filmmaking* is all the talk that has taken place and a lot of the misunderstandings about what a Zen Film is or is not. In actually, it was never my plan. I just wanted to let the concept remain wholly (or holy) Zen. But...

For better or for worse, with the passing of Donald G. Jackson, it was left to only me to define and explain the art form and philosophy known as *Zen Filmmaking*. But, the more I have written and spoken on the subject, the more I realized that people continued to use my words to feed into their own misunderstandings. From the moment I first discussed it; some people immediately got it. That was great. Others only wanted to take my words and use them as a means to criticize *Zen Filmmaking* and Zen Films. But, that's life... People like to talk and say nothing about philosophies they do not understand.

Which brings me to the point of this discourse. Finally... The ultimate truth of *Zen Filmmaking* is there are NO DEFINITIONS. A Zen Film is what it is in its own moment of time and space. Just as each film begins in the mind of the filmmaker and follows its path to creation, there is no definition or logical explanations for creativity. There is no definable reason why one person wants to create a film and another person doesn't. There is no definition for art. There is no definition for satori. As such, art and enlightenment should simply be allowed to exist within their own perfection. It is only the mind of the unenlightened that attempts to draw conclusions so that they may find a reason to love or hate a creation.

Criticizing a creation is criticizing life. Criticizing a philosophy is simply a person attempting to find fault with the spiritual understandings of another person based upon their own preconceived notions of reality.

Freedom of spirit is the true soul of *Zen Filmmaking*. *Zen Filmmaking* has no ultimate definition.

Zen Filmmaking: The Manifesto

I created *Zen Filmmaking* in 1991 as a way to make the filmmaking process as easy, as creative, and as pain free as possible. To do that, at the heart of *Zen Filmmaking* is the fact that a Zen Filmmaker does not use a script or a screenplay in the creation of a film.

The Screenplay

Many people base all of their filmmaking creativity around a screenplay and they question, *"How can you create a movie without a screenplay?"*

To answer, the reality of it is; in your mind's eye, you can write a great script. And, in that script, you have great locations, great sets, and your actors act out every word perfectly. But, the truth of independent filmmaking is, it is usually not like that.

First of all, as an independent filmmaker, you commonly do not have the money to get the locations and/or the sets that you have detailed in your screenplay. This is particularly the case if you have written an elaborate script. But, more importantly, it is quite common that due to the fact you will mostly likely be working with novice actors, they will not possess the developed ability to memorize dialogue and then speak those lines with any convincing realism. This is the reason that a large percentage of independent films are seen as unprofessional—the actors portraying their characters come off as unreal.

But now, think about this... If you have a story in mind, and I am not saying don't have a story. Because when I create a movie, I always have a story in mind. But, once you have that general storyline, instead of writing an elaborate screenplay; simply put together a cast that can bring out the essence of the characters you have in mind for your movie and then move forward and create that film.

Casting

One of the main, and most essential points of *Zen Filmmaking* to remember is, *"Your cast does not have to be professionally trained actors."* As they will not be required to memorize dialogue, (and then recite those written words with conviction), all you have to do is to gather a group of people together who look the way you want your characters to look and who can portray the emotions of the characters you have in mind for your story in the most natural manner possible.

By creating your movie with this as a basis, once you have your story, and have put together your cast, you can simply go out and find one or more locations, bring your cast to the set, and shoot your movie. It's as simple as that!

No rehearsals. Just filmmaking it is purest sense.

The Cast

I am often asked about how to best acquire a cast for a Zen Film. The main thing about casting your Zen Film is to remember, *"Some actors get it—they intrinsically understand the process of Spontaneous Creativity, and some do not."*

Most true actors actually want to improv. Why? Because by improving they get to add their own creative signature to the film.

Then, there are the ones who don't get it—the actors who must have a script. Those are the people who are really locked into different era and style of filmmaking. They want things to be fed to them. They don't want to be naturally creative.

Many people have asked me, *"What do you do with an actor or an actress who is resistant on the set?"*

To answer, *"I don't use 'em!"*

In short, find actors who are open minded to this style of natural, spontaneous creativity. If they become resistant on your set, simply ask them to leave.

As previous stated, you don't have to use professional actors!

In terms of my filmmaking, many times I'll meet a person, and they have a really interesting look or possess a very interesting personality. From this alone, I bring them on a movie and put them in the film.

...Because they don't have to memorize dialogue, they don't have to be locked into a character—they can simply be themselves. And, as stated, from this, the overall presentation of the movie, (to the audience), is much more natural.

The Crew

This, *"Naturalness,"* is the same ideology I use with my crew. You want to surround yourself with people who are creative, can think on their feet, and are not dominate by structure. You need people who are willing to change their minds at a moment's notice.

Just as with the true actor, true cinematographers and true filmmakers are always open to change and make themselves available and open to new and different inspiration.

In defining whom you should work with, the best thing to do is to meet with your crew and discuss this philosophy before you actually get out there in the trenches and are filming. Because, the fact of the matter is, you want to know that your crew is going to stand behind you once your production is in motion.

Guiding the Actor

The question is also often asked, *"If I don't use a script, how do I get my story told?"*

First of all… One of the primary understandings of *Zen Filmmaking* is, *"The stories have all been told."* If you think the story in your movie is totally original, you are lying to yourself. With this as the elemental basis, to answer the question, what I do is I get my actors on the set, I tell them what the scene is about, and I describe to them the essence of what I want them to portray or discuss in that scene. Then, I let them go at it. Many times, that is all the guidance they need, and they develop the storyline with their own unique flavor.

If, on the other hand, they need any tuning-up about the story development, I stop the scene and guide them in the direction I want the story to go. Then, I recommence shooting.

Ultimately, what happens by letting an actor be themselves is that you get a very-very natural performance. Two people, three people, four people, or however many people are in the scene, you let them talk the way they talk and develop their characters the way they develop their characters. From this, you get a very natural performance that is then presented to your audience.

Critiquing

A lot of people want to criticize independent features; whether they're No-Budget, Low-Budget, B-Movies, Cult Films, Zen Films, or whatever... But, like I always say, *"What is a film critic? With very few exceptions, a film critic is somebody who doesn't have the talent or the dedication to actually go out and make a movie."*

Because, let's face facts... Making a movie is not easy. Even with *Zen Filmmaking,* it takes a lot of focus and creative energy.

As far as the critics go, it's easy for someone to sit around and criticize films. I mean, even in the highest budget films, you can find flaws, and you can find things to criticize.

Criticizing filmmaking is very easy. But, to actually make a movie, is not easy! In fact, it's very complicated. Which again is where *Zen Filmmaking* comes into play and one of the primary reasons I created it.

Zen Filmmaking is about removing as many obstacles as possible from the filmmaking process.

Make the Mistakes Your Friend

It is essential to note, *"Obstacles,"* are the primary reason many would-be filmmakers want to start a film but never do. This is also the reason many filmmakers start to create a movie but do not complete it.

Many people start a film. But, as anybody who has ever begun walking down the road to a film's creation knows, "There will be problems!" In fact, every movie I've ever made, (and I've made a lot of 'em), there have been problems that have occurred with every single one of them. Some have been small. Some have been big. But, no film is every created without encountering some level of problems.

The fact of the matter is, you will never be able to create a movie without encountering some level of obstacles. There are going to be problems. But, *Zen Filmmaking* teaches that what you need to do is to make those obstacles part of your creative process. Like I always say, *"Make the mistakes your friend."* Because, if you, *"Make the mistakes your friend,"* then you can work within those parameters and make them part of your overall creative process.

This gets us back to the topic of other people criticizing films and, in fact, you, criticizing your own movie...

You must remember that no movie is every going to turn out exactly the way you want it to turn out. For example, as an artist, I've painted for most of my life. And, I can tell you; no painting ever turns out exactly the way I had planned.

What you need to do, in regard to the filmmaking process is, you need to understand that you have to allow a movie to be what it is. Let it be, within itself.

We all want any film we make to look a certain way and to turn out a certain way. As such, we work towards that end. That's fine. But, you cannot allow what you hope something will be, to define your movie. Things are going to happen that you are not going to like. And, if you hope to actually complete your film, instead of shutting it down and throwing in the towel during production, you have to learn to accept and live within that understanding.

Use What's Available

This brings us back to the point of, *"Make the mistakes your friend."*

With the dawning of creative and artistic movie making everything changed. Certainly, in the 1950's and 1960's, the realms of filmmaking were definitely pushed forward into the areas of the artistic and the abstract. But, I believe it was more exemplified with the dawning of the age of music videos.

What happened was, with the birth of artistic filmmaking, (and music videos are just that), there came to be a new and expanded understanding that a film can be as abstract as you want them to be. Colors can be anything. Scenes can be anything. Your cuts can be as erratic as you desire them to be. So, instead of becoming upset with your project if you find unexpected flaws, make all of that a part of your filmmaking process and use it as an actual signature for the film you are creating.

Certainly, you try to get a scene looking the way you want it to look. But, if it doesn't happen, allow yourself to be free and creative enough to be able to use the elements and the things that are available to us now in order to complete your film.

Early in the Game

When I first began making films, we were shooting on actual film, and it was very-very expensive. You had to buy the film. You had to develop the film. Then, you had to make copies of the film so you could edit the movie. This was done because you did not want to damage your original footage. So, you either copied the film to a work-print or you transferred the film to video with timecode where it was then edited on Three Quarter Inch Masters or Beta Masters. Then, after you completed the edit, you would *Telecine* the film to correct minor color or lighting imperfections. This process, at its cheapest, cost one-hundred dollars an hour.

With *Telecine* you could somewhat change the overall look of the film. If it was a little dark, you could bring up the light. If it was little light, you could bring it down. And, you could change the overall color texture of the film to a certain degree. But, for the most part, you were left with what you had shot.

Today, you can do all of these lighting and color correction and more on your computer. But, even with this ability, your film is probably not going to be the exact way you may have envisioned it to be. Your D.P. may have shot certain scenes a little dark. He, (or she), may have shot them a little light. The scenes may be out of focus. Or, there may be some audio problems. But, these factors should not be a reason to stop you or stop the film!

What I am saying is to take all of those elements: out of focus, poor lighting, color variations, whatever, make them a part of your creative, finished product.

If you have to add coloration to your film or if you have to make it black and white instead of color, do it! Use all of the things at your disposal to get your finished product out there!

That is the ultimate lesson of *Zen Filmmaking.* Make a movie and get it out there!

Make the Process Happen

In short, in *Zen Filmmaking,* what you do is to start out with a story. Then, you go out there and film it. When you look at your competed footage, if it's not quite what you expected, that's fine. It's all part of the process.

From making a movie in this manner you can learn while you get a new film out there. Then, in your next movie, you will understand, *"Well... I made a little miscalculation doing that on my last film, so I won't do it again. I didn't like what happened when I did that, so I'm going to do it a different way this time."*

From all of these experiences, the next time you make a film, it will be so much better. And that's the ultimate thing about filmmaking – doing it, completing a project, and getting it out there as a calling card. Getting it out there to entertain the masses.

Removing the Obstacles

As stated, the main thing about *Zen Filmmaking* is that it's about removing as many obstacles as possible from the filmmaking process. It's about being as spontaneous as possible.

What that means is that you don't want to lock yourself into a highly defined mindset—full of preconceived definitions. You want to leave your mind open so that you can adapt to new creative ideas and experiences when they present themselves to you.

For example, when I go out and shoot a movie, I have my cast, and I have some ideas of where I am going to shoot. But, if I see a new location while driving and think, *"Wow, this would really work in the film,"* we get out of the car and we go and do one or more scenes at the location.

And, the fact of the matter is, you never know what's going to happen. This is why in *Zen Filmmaking* we don't use scripts. Because with no script, you are allowed to be free in your own, *"Spontaneous Creation."* So, if I see a location, my cast and crew are allowed to go there and film. That's where the magic of *Zen Filmmaking* happens. You don't lock yourself into a structured process.

Structure

For the filmmakers who still desire some form and structure in the filmmaking process, I can tell them what I do while creating one of my Zen Films. First, I have a shot list. Each day, I create a shot list of the scenes I want to have happen for the movie. Then, I allow freedom and the magic of Zen to take over. So, if we are driving along, we see a location, we get out, and we'll film a scene or two. Maybe it works, maybe it doesn't. But, what I come away with is at least a few more minutes of footage that will add to the overall production value of the film.

In independent filmmaking, you commonly don't have the money to go out and reshoot a scene if it does not come out as you had planned. On multi-million-dollar films, (and as an actor I've worked on several of them), the filmmakers can go back to the location; they can bring back the entire cast and crew, and re-film scenes if they don't like the way they turned out. In fact, I have been in movies where million-dollar scenes were completely cut out of the final film. But, on the independent level, you really can't do that. So, what you want to do is to be as free, as spontaneous, as creative, and as in-the-moment as possible. From this, you allow yourself to take advantage of whatever is happening. If you see a location, go film there. If the sun is setting and the light's getting low; okay, you add that to your movie. If the sun's coming up or if it's a bright sunny day or if it starts to rain, add all that to the story development of your film.

From shooting a film in this fashion you add to the overall production value and presentation of your movie. Plus, you present your audience with additional depth to your stories and your character's development.

There are three man points to remember in Zen Filmmaking:

1. Don't lock yourself into a script.

2. Don't lock yourself into locations.

3. Bring a cast and a crew on board who get the idea of, *"Spontaneous Creativity."*

From this, everything becomes free. It becomes easy. It becomes, for lack of a better term, *"A spiritual process of filmmaking."*

Like I always say, *"Zen Filmmaking leads to Cinematic Enlightenment."* What does that mean? It means by being free, by allowing the natural flow of creativity to guide you and your process, your film become as natural, as free, and as spiritual as possible. And from that, true art can be lived and created.

Zen Filmmaking
Understanding the Cinematic Art

I think it is almost essential that I write a few words about *Zen Filmmaking* its origin, and just what is or is not a Zen Film. This is due to the fact that over the past few years I have been deluged with questions about the essence and the truth of *Zen Filmmaking.*

Mostly, these few words are for those of you who have heard about *Zen Filmmaking* somewhere on the internet, or from a friend, and have not read my book on the subject, *Zen Filmmaking,* which pretty much spells it all out from A to Z.

History

The birth of *Zen Filmmaking* came about when Donald G. Jackson and I were making the film *The Roller Blade Seven* in 1991. *The Roller Blade Seven* began in much the same way as most films. Don had obtained financing for a film, and he wanted to continue the concept he had developed in his film *Roller Blade* and its sequel *Roller Blade Warriors.* He wanted to take the concept to the next level and create a martial art driven epic film. He asked me to come on board, co-produce, co-write, choreograph the martial arts, and star in the film. Upon our entering into pre-production, our Executive Producer wanted to see what we planned to film. So, Don asked me to write a screenplay – which I did. If you would like to read this screenplay you can pick up my book, *The Screenplays.*

The impetus for the birth of *Zen Filmmaking* occurred after the first weekend of production on *The Roller Blade Seven*. Don and I were very disappointed with the performances of the massive cast we had hired to take part in the film. We looked at each other and realized that the majority of them did not have the talent to truly pull-off the roll of the character they had been assigned. With this, we came to a realization to just go out and film the movie, not expect anything from our cast and crew, and make up the story as we went along. After a few days of this style of production, I had a realization, based in my lifelong involvement with eastern mysticism. I looked at Don and said, *"This is Zen. This is Zen Filmmaking."* And, that was it. That was the creation of the term, the title, and the style. *Zen Filmmaking* was born. And, from that moment forward, I began to define and refine *Zen Filmmaking*—making it both an Art Form and a Science. From that point onward I have moved forward and continued to refine the process of *Zen Filmmaking.*

After we completed *The Roller Blade Seven* and its sequel *Return of the Roller Blade Seven*, Don and I went our separate ways for several years. I immediately went into production on the Zen Film, *Samurai Vampire Bikers from Hell*. Don returned to predominantly screenplay-based productions. In 1996 we reconnected and again set on the path of *Zen Filmmaking*, as a team. From this, we created a number of Zen Films together.

Just What is a Zen Film?

Many people believe that *Zen Filmmaking* is simply based upon the fact that no screenplay is used in the creation of a Zen Film. Though this is the basis for *Zen Filmmaking,* in reality it is much more than this.

Many people ask, *"Why no script?"* Well, there are a few reasons for this. First of all, and perhaps most importantly, from a philosophic perspective, screenplays keep you locked into a stagnate mindset. If your film is created around a screenplay, then your cast and crew are very reluctant to allow things to change. But, if you go into a project with simply an overview of a story idea, then your project becomes free and new inspiration is allowed to occur at any moment. And, believe me, from someone who has made a lot of films, you never know what new inspiration will strike or what GREAT unexpected situation will present itself when you get to your location, have your cast in place, and are open minded about what you will actually film.

The other reason to not use a screenplay is based upon the fact that in your mind's eye you can write a great story, have it set in elaborate locations, and acted out by great actors. For anyone who has ever been on a low-budget movie set, you quickly see that this is not the case. So, what occurs by writing an elaborate screenplay is that you are only setting yourself up for disappointment. But, with no screenplay, you are free. Any production is allowed to happen as it happens and become what it becomes.

The Six Tenets of Zen Filmmaking

Though *Zen Filmmaking* is based upon the concepts of creative freedom and cinematic spontaneity, this does not mean that *Zen Filmmaking* has no foundational elements. To help define *Zen Filmmaking*, I designed, *The Six Tenets of Zen Filmmaking.* They are:

1. Make all unpredicted situations work to your advantage.

2. Don't waste time, money, and energy attempting to create your sets when you don't have to. Instead, travel to them and allow their natural aesthetics to become a part of your film.

3. Just do it! Ninety-nine percent of the time you can get away with it.

4. Never let your storyline dominate your artistic vision. Too many would be filmmakers attempt to write what they believe is a, *"Good Script,"* and then try to film it. Without an unlimited budget it is virtually impossible to get what is on the page on the stage.

5. *Zen Filmmaking* is a spontaneous process. Just as the Zen understanding of enlightenment teaches that though you may meditate for years, it is not until the moment when you step beyond your thinking mind and realize that you are already enlightened that you achieve Satori. Thus, if you acutely plan your productions, with screenplays, storyboards, and locations, there is no room for the instantaneousness of Cinematic

Enlightenment to occur, and you will always be lost between the way your mind desired a scene to be and the way it actually turns out.

6. Ultimately, in *Zen Filmmaking* nothing is desired and, thus, all outcomes are perfect.

Make it Your Own!
I am continually asked, *"What do I think about other people making films and calling them Zen Films?"* Or, *"What do I think about people using my concept of Zen Filmmaking."* To answer, I think it's great! The entire reason I have continued to focus on *Zen Filmmaking,* for so many years, is to make the process of filmmaking easier, more joyous, and provide all filmmakers, (not only myself), with a means of creating a film while encountering the minimal number of disappointments with the finished product.

So, if you want to call your film a Zen Film, do it! That's fine with me.

Moreover, make *Zen Filmmaking* your own. There are no hard and fast rules in *Zen Filmmaking.* I frequently receive questions asking if it is okay to change the process a little bit. As I always answer, *"Of course, do what works for you. Make Zen Filmmaking your own! Take my philosophies and alter them to work for you, your film, and your filmmaking situation."*

Donald G. Jackson and Me
I often receive e-mails from people assuming that all of the films Donald G. Jackson were Zen Films. This is not the case. Though my meeting and filmmaking collaborations with

Donald G. Jackson set the course of *Zen Filmmaking* into motion, he was not the creator of *Zen Filmmaking.* That was me. In fact, virtually all of the films he created, that I was not directly associated with, were screenplay-based productions. And, this is in direct contrast to the primary premise of *Zen Filmmaking*—that no screenplay should be used in the creation of a film. So, all of you people out there who are discussing the fact that films like *Hell Comes to Frogtown, Return to Frogtown, Roller Blade, Roller Blade Warriors,* and even such obscure Donald G. Jackson directed films such as *Rollergator* and *Big Sister 2000* are Zen Films, you are incorrect. These films were all script-based films that were written by one of Donald G. Jackson's friends, most notably Randy Frakes or Mark Williams.

Critique

From the questions I receive about *Zen Filmmaking,* I have come to realize that there is a big misconception about the reasoning behind *Zen Filmmaking* and the actual method used in this style of cinematic creation. Mostly I have come to understand that many people just don't get it. Most people assume that simply because the process of *Zen Filmmaking* is a script-less form of cinematic creation, that means that a Zen Film is simply a mishmash of image and scenes strung together. And, people have used this misunderstanding as a means for criticizing Zen Films. They are really missing the point. Though there are no scripts used in a Zen Film, the process of creating a Zen Film is a very conscious process—a process that very few filmmakers could, in fact, ever employ due to the fact that it is a very refined method of filmmaking that is complicated in its simplicity. That is a very Zen statement, I know. But, the abstract nature of Zen is at the heart of *Zen Filmmaking.* Most people need structure and guidelines, but structure and guidelines are never relied upon in *Zen Filmmaking.*

Imagine, having the mental focus, as a filmmaker, to create a film that tells a story and do so without any written dialogue or scene descriptions. Just like *Zazen,* (Zen meditation), the focus it takes to create a Zen Film is a refined/developed ability that few people have the mental wherewithal to achieve.

Though the essence of *Zen Filmmaking* is based upon the understanding of never relaying upon the formalized structure of using a script, or any other limiting method of story dissemination to create a film for that matter, there is much more to *Zen Filmmaking* than simply that. At the heart of *Zen Filmmaking* is the spiritual essence of Zen—understanding that all life is a pathway to *Nirvana.* And, that we ALL are already enlightened—we simply need to realize it. Therefore, in truth, *Zen Filmmaking* is not simply a process of filmmaking. It is, in fact, a formalized practice of meditation leading to cinematic enlightenment. How do you achieve this? Let go and you will know.

This being stated, if you want to read a more nuts-and-bolts on-line article about *Zen Filmmaking,* you can read my article, *Just do it! The Art of Zen Filmmaking* in the book *Zen Filmmaking* or @ scottshaw.com.

I trust these words will more precisely explain the essence of *Zen Filmmaking* for those of you have wondered. For everyone else, either read the book or keep the questions coming. I will try to answer them as best as I can...

Zen Filmmaking
and the Philosophy of Filmmaking

There are a lot of people that want to make movies. I meet people all the time that talk about making a film. Very few of them actually move forward and complete a film, however.

Even in the classes I have taught on filmmaking at various colleges and universities, very few of the students follow through with their desire. In fact, I have taught classes at one or two universities where the school supplied cameras, sound, and lighting equipment. But, only maybe a third of the class got out there and tried to complete a project.

There are also a lot of gung-ho want-to-be filmmakers out there who are influenced by and want to make movies like, John Woo, Quentin Tarantino, Robert Rodriguez, or Martin Scorsese. That's great! But, the problem exists that if a person doesn't have a lot of money, it is very hard to make a movie to the level of those filmmakers. Very few can mimic these filmmaker's early works and create a project as compelling as they did with a limited budget.

This gets me to philosophy. People wish to make grandiose films—though some will deny this fact. They want to make movies that look big. But, if one is tied down by a limited budget, which equals a less than tired and professional cast and crew, small will very rarely equal big.

It is for this reason that before a new filmmaker enters the game and encounters disappointments that leads to production shutdown, they need to cultivate their own philosophy about how to deal with the limitations of a limited budget.

The fact is, unless you have a lot of money, there will be disappointments. And, disappointments are the number one cause of people throwing in the towel.

For me, it was just a natural progression to come to define *Zen Filmmaking*. Through my experiences in life and particularly in art and living in Asia, it was simply an expression of my understanding of life.

I am happy if it helps you and you employee *Zen Filmmaking*. But, I understand, *Zen Filmmaking* is not for everyone. This is why novice filmmakers need to come up with their own filmmaking strategy. They need to do this in order to be able to consciously overcome the obstacles and the disappointments. And, there will be obstacles and the disappointments.

I cannot emphasize this enough. Because I meet so many people that want to make films but never get one completed because they do not go into the process with a philosophic strategy.

Formulate what works best for you. And, make your films.

Zen Filmmaking X 2 or 3

I often receive questions from people who are attempting to make a movie and two or more of the primary filmmakers are having conflicts. These people want to know how can they make a movie if they are frequently at odds with the other filmmaker; who is oftentimes a good friend or a family member. I have discussed this issue in two of my books, *Zen Filmmaking* and more specifically in, *Independent Filmmaking: Secrets of the Craft.* But, in brief, my belief is that there can only be one *Captain of the Ship* on any film project or things can get very messy.

That being said, there is another alternative. That other alternative is to allow the two or more filmmakers to go their separate ways. This is to say, allow the one, two, or three filmmakers involved with the project to go off and film the scenes they want to film in the style and manner in which they want them to be created. Then, when filming is complete, bring the various footage together and edit into one movie.

This style of multi-filmmaker filmmaking can be orchestrated in a couple of different ways. One, you can have a script and/or a story idea with a shot list and then divide the scenes between the two or more filmmakers. Each then goes out with their cast and crew and gets the footage shot. In this way, there is no conflict as no filmmaker is stepping on the toes of another filmmaker's style.

The other way to do this, (and the way I prefer), is to simply have an end-point story idea in mind, that you have discussed with the other involved filmmakers, and then go off and get the movie shot. For this specific filmmaking process to work, the filmmakers should define a timeframe: be it a day, two days, a week, or whatever. Then, do not even discuss what the other person or persons plan to do. Just go out a do it. At the end of your shooting schedule, you then come together and, in many cases, you will be amazed at what the other person has created. From this, you will have created a truly unique film and will not have encountered interpersonal conflict.

Now, I am not saying that this is the perfect method to make a multi-filmmaker film. There can be jealousies over the finished product, (as one person may be considered by the other person to have done a better job), one person may be behind schedule, over budget, or it is believed that one person really messed up, etcetera… But, for multi-filmmakers who actually wish to make a film together this can be a very unique and creative process to get a film finished without enduring internal struggle.

A side-note here is: You can also do this if you are two filmmakers in different cities, states, or even in different countries. Simply get a story idea that you both agree upon and go out and shoot the film in your specific location. Then, you can either send the footage to one or the other person to edit or you can each edit your own footage and put the two edited segments together. From this, BAM you have created a truly unique multi-filmmaker film.

Zen Filmmaking:
Process Verse Product

It seems that there is no way that I can ever discuss *Zen Filmmaking* without speaking of Donald G. Jackson. And, that is not bad thing for without him having the deal in place for us to make *Roller Blade Seven* I may never have come up with the philosophic ideology for the process and continued forward with making Zen Films.

After Don's passing, I was helping his wife clear out some of the tons of things Don had collected – as she and his daughter were moving from the house they had lived in for over twenty years. Don was a terrible hoarder. Oh, I mean collector…

In any case, we found something that referenced *Zen Filmmaking*. She handed it to me and said, *"I guess this is for you, as you're the source."* I smiled, "That's me…"

But, it is much more complicated than that. *Zen Filmmaking* really goes to the source and the difference(s) between who Don and I are and were as human beings. Don was very explosive, egocentric, a total power tripper—he did not care about most people; their feelings or their thoughts. Though he did spend a lot of money on his young want-a-be starlet paramours, getting them boob jobs and paying their rent. His payment was retuned by… Well, you can figure it out.

Working with Don was always both a blessing and a curse. On one hand he was a total hustler, so we had some high budgets for our films. In fact, on one of the last big galas before he died, *Demon Lover Diary* showed at the DGA, Director's Guild of America, here in L.A. I thought it was a great blessing from the beyond as Don got a lot of press surrounding that event and this happened as he was getting very sick and closely approaching the end of his life—though I and his direct family were the only ones who knew this. After the screening they asked him to do a Q & A. One of things he said to describe himself was, *"I used to be an artist, now I'm just a guy who asks other people for money."* Sad but true.

And, I guess that leads to the point of this writing. Yes, Don was a filmmaker. And, I believe a truly revolutionary, artistic one. But, he was more into the process then the product. I mean, we would hang out everyday. We would meet at our offices in North Hollywood, do casting sessions, eat burgers, (Don's favorite food), hang out with young actresses, go to invitation only industry private screenings, go and see obscure Blue Grass, Folk, and Alt Country bands at night; but rarely would we film. Maybe once or twice a week we would actually break out the cameras and get something done.

For example, it took us *months-upon-*months to film RB7. *Guns of El Chupacabra* went on for over a year. I remember when we were filming the scenes at the *Cinco de Mayo* (5th of May) celebration I looked at Don and said, *"Remember, we started filming this over a year ago in January?"*

That was just the way it was with him. Then, once we did have enough footage, he would hide it away until it was an absolute necessity to finish it before he would turn it over to me to edit.

This is also why soon before he passed away, when he was in the hospitable, he made sure his wife turned all our footage over to me; as there were so many films yet to be edited. I immediately started and did my duty. That is why more films involving Donald G. Jackson came out after his death than while he was alive.

There was always a price to pay for working with Don. I said that while he was alive, (to his face), and after he died. Though I covered the process of *Roller Blade Seven,* the first Zen Film, pretty well in a chapter in my book, *Zen Filmmaking,* I think that it is almost necessary that, at some point, I write a second chapter, *Roller Blade Seven: The Darkness in the Light,* because a lot of bad things happened in association with that film, intermixed with the good things.

In fact, the very first day on the very first set that involved Don and I—the film was *Roller Blade Three,* our course of events was set in motion. I had met Don shortly before that and he had asked me to star in the film. I arrived on the set, as did all of the rest of the cast and the crew. The female lead asked me if I wanted to run our lines, as it was a script-based production. I said, *"No, I don't really do that. Let's just wait till we get on set and let it happen."* See... I was *Zen Filmmaking* before there was *Zen Filmmaking.*

After that, I went looking for Don. He was outside, taking all of the junk he had in the trunk of his 1962 Plymouth out and placing it on the ground. *"Just thought I would get this all in order,"* he stated. He was doing this while the cast and crew meandered around with no direction.

The film never got completed. Though I plan to do a documentary about this film with the behind-the-scenes footage at some point.

I always believe that life provides you with signs as what is to come. In the case of Donald G. Jackson, as he worked with his trunk while the cast and crew had no idea what to do, my first thought was to bail that fiasco—as up until that point in my career I had been working on high-budget or at least very organized productions. But, I stayed and it led to what it led to... *Zen Filmmaking.*

Am I sorry I stayed? No, not at all. But, as stated, there was always a price to pay working with Don and sometimes that price was quite high.

In closing, Don and I were very *yin and yang* – very different parts of the same puzzle. Me, I am about completion. I like to get it done. ...Because then you have accomplished something. Don was not like that.

Life is always a battle between, process verse product. Spiritually commonly provides people with the excuse, *"Enjoy the process."* Sure, enjoy it, but many people use that as a life-excuse for not making things happen and getting things done.

If you don't get it done, it is not done. Then, what have you accomplished?

So, if I must state one firm premise of *Zen Filmmaking,* that premise is, in *Zen Filmmaking* you get your project completed.

Zen Filmmaking and What is a Zen Film?

Ever since I created *Zen Filmmaking*, I have frequently been asked the question, *"Just what is a Zen Film?"* Numerous people have contacted me regarding this question, and I have read a number of attempts by people to write a formalized definition. Some have been good while others have placed far too much analysis into the process. But to answer, I think, first-and-foremost, it is essential to note that the ultimate understanding of Zen is that there is no absolute definition—no one truth. This is the first clue into what is or is not a Zen Film.

But, to provide a more detailed explanation...

At the root of a Zen Film and *Zen Filmmaking* is the understanding that, *"The stories have all been told."* I say this over and over again, but people still don't get it. So, let me explain...

Think about it, every story throughout humanity has previously either been written about or filmed. Certainly, there are some very specific variants of life-stories that may seem a bit more unique than others, but these minor variations are not the only time that these life events have occurred.

Take a look at the bible. Every storyline is in that ancient text—from romance to horror, onto science fiction. It is very hard to find any story of humanity that is not alluded to in the bible.

But, why does this matter? And, how does this help to define a Zen Film?

Filmmakers, from the dawning of the craft foreword, have attempted to tell a story. Many become very adamant about how elementally important the story is to their film. They equally believe that it is very important that their film's particular story must be told. So, they go and make a movie. Maybe it is good, maybe it is bad. But, ultimately, it is certainly not a story that has never been told before.

You may ask, *"Why is this important in defining a Zen Film?"* Because *Zen Filmmaking* is about freedom. A Zen Film is about freeing yourself from as many constraints as possible. And certainly, the story or the script is one of the most limiting factors in any film's production.

Why is freedom essential in making a Zen Film? Because then the filmmaking process becomes much more spontaneous, natural, and artistic. And, when freedom is allowed to exist, then true art is embraced.

Which brings me to the concept of Art...

There are beautiful paintings that have been created since the dawning evolution of humanity where the artists have studied for years, refined their techniques, and then spent weeks, months, even years creating a singular piece of art. Are these pieces of art beautiful? Well, if you like that style of art, then yes, they are.

Now, here arises one of the key concepts in defining a Zen Film. Just like beauty, art is in the eye of the beholder.

To some, classic art is the only art. But, to others, this style of art has all been seen before. It has become old and expected.

In regard to filmmaking, the same understanding applies. So many filmmakers, especially on the independent level, attempt to create a film that looks much bigger than its budget—they attempt to mimic what has been done before. Though they most probably believe that they have a unique story that deserves telling, what they are doing is no more than retelling the same story that was most probably better told in a previous film that had a much higher budget.

Let's think about this. What if you release yourself from this whole process? What if you remove the obstacle of a highly developed story that took you months or years to write? What if you remove the need for training and simply step into the arena of filmmaking and create? What occurs? Art is what occurs.

Now, I am not saying that everybody will appreciate a film created in this style—created from a mindset of freedom. But, you can find mistakes in even the most expensive films if you look for them and certainly those films are criticized, as well. So, a Zen Film, as it is created with art as its core, can be expected to find criticism. But, the Zen Filmmaker maintains the mindset that this is all part of the package and welcomes it as it simply reveals the limited understanding of those individuals applying said criticism.

A Zen Film embraces art at its most elemental level. Is everybody going to like it? No. Does everybody like the paintings of the abstractionists or the neo-expressionists? No, they don't. Art is in the eye of the beholder! So, to make art, you will find your critics. But, who are these people that are criticizing the filmmaking of others? Are they artists? Are they making films? Most probably not.

From a personal perspective, as an artist, someone who paints, I can tell you that no painting ever turns out exactly like you expected. This is the same with film. Yet, many filmmakers have a concept locked firmly into their mind and they write and rewrite, film and refilm, attempting to get an exact mental image on the screen. But, it will never happen. What will happen from following this process of filmmaking, however, is a lot of anxiety, frustration, and discontentment. Each of these things can cause a filmmaker to toss in the towel and never complete their film. So, stop it! Allow your mistakes to become part of your film. Because, in fact, there is no such thing as a mistake, it is simply the perfection of the way it turned out. Remove expectation from your life and your film and you become free.

This brings me to the next point in detailing a Zen Film, *"Trust the Zen."*

What is the Zen? The Zen is allowing things to happen that are unexpected. The Zen is allowing the greater good of art and the positive forces of the universe to bring you things that were never expected: be these people, locations, or ideas to help you make your film the most perfect and complete that it can be.

Remove yourself and your desired outcome from the equitation. Turn off your controlling ego. Let your actors act. Let your crew do what they do. And, be open to new inspiration and change and you will encounter elements in your filmmaking process that will astonish you. This is a Zen Film.

Finally, as alluded to in the beginning, there is no absolute definition as to what is or is not a Zen Film. A Zen Film is based in freedom, not definition. A Zen Film is based in art, not structure. It is simply what comes out at the end of a particular film's evolution when you allow the natural process of creativity to take its course, and you allow your film to be.

Freedom is Art. Art is Zen.

Zen Filmmaking: Now and Zen

Zen Filmmaking has gone through a lot of evolution since I first came up with the title and concept while Donald G. Jackson and I were making, *The Roller Blade Seven* back in 1991.

Though there has been a lot of criticism of that movie, I think all that is *very-very* funny. Some people just don't get that we knew what we were doing. And, as I have stated time-and-time again, we did what we did very consciously. We meant to make that movie and the sequel the way we did.

One the other side, there are a lot of people, who really dig the film. They get what we were doing. That's life...

Anyway, as many of you know, at the heart of *Zen Filmmaking* is allowing actors to deliver their lines and develop their characters via guided improv. One of the main things to realize about *Zen Filmmaking,* particularly regarding, *Roller Blade Seven*, is that there was very little improv in that movie. That is except for much of the dialogue delivered by Joe Estevez and Don Stroud. In fact, most of the lines spoken were fed to the actors by Don or myself. Back then, Don and I didn't trust that most of the people could deliver their lines with any believability, if they were allowed to improv. So, we told them what to say.

One of the greatest exchanges of the film, *"You mean my sister that became your sister? Yes, our sister, sister..."* Don and I had come up with while eating burgers at *Tommy's* in Granada Hills just prior to filming Frank Stallone. We had gone there to write down what dialogue he should deliver, and we came up with the scene where

Don and my character interact in the film for the first time.

This trend of feeding lines followed through to *Samurai Vampire Bikers from Hell*. There was very little actual improv in that film. My friend and co-filmmaker on that feature, Kenneth H. Kim, and I came up with virtually all of the dialogue in that movie and then I pretty much fed everyone, everything.

Ken, who was a budding screenwriter, wanted to write some of the dialogue. Though that is not in the tradition of *Zen Filmmaking;* as a friend, I let him have at it. And then, I let some of the more experienced actors in the film work from that premises.

The greatest dialogue exchange of that film, I believe, is when in the opening of the film an actress, Kimberly Bolin, exclaims, *"I thought you guys were going to take me to Hollywood!"* The response, *"Hollywood... Hollywood's just a state of mind."* That was a little ditty I had come up with on the spot and gave it to the actors.

A memorable line, that I think really sets the tone of the film...

Don liked to call himself a *Zen Filmmaker*. And, certainly without our interaction, *Zen Filmmaking* may never have occurred. But, in the films he made, where I was not involved, he virtually always based the film upon a script. Then, he would let some of the actors add their own interpretation.

As I've continued as a filmmaker, since the days of RB7 and SV, I have continued to evolve the concept of *Zen Filmmaking*. What I have found is that if I surround myself with actors who can do what they do very believably—if they can be themselves. Then, they can really deliver a very natural performance. From this, the concept of improv has continued to grow in my films. I get good people and then I let them run with it...

Recently, when I was speaking with a potential actress, she asked me, *"Does it always work?"* No, it does not. There have been a few times when, mostly due to a person's ego, I have had to pull the plug and recast. But, it is rare.

The funny think about *Zen Filmmaking* and its evolution is, most people have never seen my films that I believe are ideal examples of *Zen Filmmaking*. Films like: *The Hard Edge of Hollywood, Blood on the Guitar, Killer: Dead or Alive, Undercover X, Hitman City, Super Hero Central, Vampire Blvd.,* or *Vampire Noir*. Most, have based all of their appraisal of *Zen Filmmaking* upon seeing, *The Roller Blade Seven*. Which, even I will tell you, was designed to be STRANGE.

I guess, whatever... That's life. But, FYI, *Zen Filmmaking* has, and continues, to evolve.

Zen Filmmaking
and the Non-Narrative Film

At the heart of *Zen Filmmaking* is the ideology that, "The stories have all been told." Therefore, why attempt to tell the same story that has been filmed a thousand times, over-and-over again, simply by providing it with a different title?

This is one of the primary reasons why in *Zen Filmmaking* we do not use scripts. Though the Zen Filmmaker may begin with an overview of a story concept, they allow the naturalness of non-defined organic, spiritual inspiration to be the only guide in the formation of the Zen Film. As nothing is etched in stone, (i.e., no script), the Zen Film is allowed to develop in a natural and unhindered process. From this, the Zen Filmmaker frees themselves from the constraints of a formalized story and enters into the world of artistic cinematic creation. By allowing the film to evolve in its own naturalness during the filming and particularity the editing process, many a Zen Film has been created.

There have been many Zen Film created with this technique as a foundation. But, the next evolution of *Zen Filmmaking* is the non-narrative film.

What is a non-narrative film? With no need to tell a story, an entire film is simply allowed to be what it is—constructed with film footage the Zen Filmmaker deems appropriate to edit into one cohesive product.

No story need be told, as all the stories have already been told. No definitions of filmmaking particulars need to be defined: such as a particular filming technique, delineated lighting, specific character development, or formalized editing. The footage that is shot is allowed to be what it is and is then put together via the freedom based, ongoing cinematic vision of the filmmaker.

Freedom is the essence of Zen. The non-narrative Zen Film is, therefore, the absolute embodiment of Zen.

SECTION II: Q & A
Zen Filmmaking:
Questions and Correspondence

Q&A

I frequently receive questions about Zen Filmmaking and how to make a Zen Film. I always try to focus on the specific question(s) that people ask and provide specific answers.

As I receive so many questions from people who are trying to make a film and as there are so many other people out there who wish to do the same but are running into problems, I try to put some of these encapsulated answers out there in order to help in the process of getting your film completed.

Sometimes I receive general questions that go to the essential understandings of Zen Filmmaking, sometimes they are much broader. Following are answers to various question of the subject of filmmaking and Zen Filmmaking which will perhaps help you understand the process of getting your film made and getting it out there.

Zen Filmmaking: The Process in a Nutshell

Dear Dr. Shaw,

I am an aspiring independent filmmaker and last night I was reading about Zen filmmaking, and it fascinated me, but I do not understand how your films can look and seem so well done when there was no script involved. How do you make a good Zen Film?

Hi,

That is a bit of a complicated question but in brief... *Zen Filmmaking* is about making the movie you want to make in the most stress free, natural, and dare I say, spiritual, manner possible. How do you do this? You just get out there and do it.

But, the fact of the matter is, to make a movie look good, especially on a low or no budget level takes practice. You have to know what you are doing. You have to understanding lighting, you have to understand how to use your camera, and you have to know how to get good sound. How do you master these techniques; by doing it!

As for the script, if you've read about *Zen Filmmaking*, then you know that we believe a script simply hinders the process. Why? Because it keeps you locked into a mindset of what must be said and what must be done. This robs creative freedom and causes problems because everyone expects something to happen. Then, if it doesn't happen or if it looks bad once it is filmed, everyone becomes unhappy.

What do I use instead of a script? What I do is to make up a shot list of what I hope to do each day. Then, I just let it happen. If it stays the same; great! If everything changes, also great!

When we are about to film a scene, I tell the actors the basic premise of what they are supposed to convey and then I let them speak in their own voice. By doing it this way, all the performances become very natural.

As I have discussed many times, *Zen Filmmaking* is not for everybody. Like meditation, it takes a lot of focused energy. But, the people who have delved into it, and made it their own, universally come to love the process.

Hope this helps…

All the best,
S.

Zen Filmmaking:
Questions and Correspondence Long-Form

Here is an e-mail discussion on filmmaking, and particularly Zen Filmmaking, that I've had with a young filmmaker.

Over the past year or so he has asked several very interesting questions and has described his experiences in relation to filmmaking and Zen Filmmaking.

As the questions answered, and his experiences detailed, may be of help to other filmmakers, I thought I would provide this ongoing discussion in order to possibly alleviate some of the obstacles in the filmmaking process for those of you who are interested.

19 June 2009

Hi, my name is J. I e-mailed you about a month ago, and your reply was very encouraging. Right now, I'm in the process of shooting my first feature film. The title is called, "Monique" and its a coming-of-age drama of a teenage girl trying to fit into a group of popular girls. I still can't believe it. But your book has inspired me more than any other filmmaking book. Anyways, I hope I'm not taking too much of your time, but I wanted to let you know this:

When I started this movie, I did write a script, since the cast was requesting at least some written thing to get started. So, I wrote a very loose forty page script with a little bit of dialogue, but it helped me sort of organize the movie and find out how many locations, etc. However, while I'm still in the process of pre-production, as I was looking for locations, I came to this really interesting... I guess, "Revelation," Scott Shaw was right! I can't use a script, it's too limiting! When I finally traveled to the locations, they didn't look like the ones I envisioned in my mind. So I just simply let go of the script and secured 4 locations and let the rest come up as we are in the, "Process of Creation." Also, my main actors wanted a rehearsal, so we went to a coffee shop, and I had them go through the script. The dialogue sounded forced and dull, since none of them are professional or Hollywood actors. So, I told them to just go with the flow and use your feelings to convey the aspects of the scene. I couldn't believe it! They were naturally doing everything and more than what I had intended. So, all in all, you are right. For a no-budget indie film, a script seems useless.

Also, I like how in your book, "Zen Filmmaking," you say that you put as much creativity in all the aspects of the production as possible. When I was doing lighting tests for my film, my DP wanted it to look natural, but when we finally looked at the tape we were both disappointed at how digital video looks in natural lighting. So, I gelled the hell out of the lights, bounced them off at random points on the walls, and then added fog. When we looked at the tape again, we were both impressed. Even though it wasn't natural it was creative and looked more, "Movie-like," than the natural lighting.

Thank you, Scott Shaw for inspiring me to, "Trust my feelings," and my guts. I'm in my last year at the Arizona State University film program, and all I can say is film school can be very limiting on *personal vision. I still don't know why not as many people have heard of you or your book.*

Anyways, I also had a question: What is different about your new book on filmmaking than, "Zen Filmmaking?" Because I'm planning on buying your new one, but the first was awesome as it is.

Thanks,
J.

Hi J,

Thanks for the nice e-mail. I'm glad my thoughts on filmmaking have helped you out.

And remember; just make *Zen Filmmaking* your own. Work out what works best for you, your cast and your crew, and make cinema magic!!!

Re: Your question about my new book on Independent Filmmaking.

The book is different... It is more focused on some of the general tricks of the trade rather than on the philosophically based *Zen Filmmaking*. It is more, *"In your face,"* if you will. Though my ideologies in the book are the same, it does discuss how the filmmakers can overcome additional obstacles, and it does detail different behind the scenes stories, etc.

All the best,
S.

14 April 2010

To: Dr. Shaw

    Hello, this is J. I think it has been almost a year since I last e-mailed you (it's amazing how time flies). First, I just want to say, I cannot thank you enough for your books and inspiration. Honestly, at first, I was a little skeptical about Zen filmmaking, but being an aspiring no budget filmmaker with little money, I just decided to go over the cliff and, "Just Do It!" last year. Well, my film is now completed, and I even made a good friend who was an actor in my production who wants to star in my next movie. I can't believe it! I have also bought your book Independent Filmmaking: secrets of the craft, and that one is better than the last one. I wish though I had read that before the production of, "Monique," but I'm planning on using your great tips and inspiration for my next movie. Here are just a few things I'd like to share with you that I wasn't prepared for while making my little $2,000 movie:

1. The film turned out very, very different from how I envisioned it. It looked, not surprisingly enough, like a $2,000 home movie. Even though I shot 9 hour's worth of footage, much of it was unusable, or just plain boring, so when I finally cut it down, I ended up with a 50-minute film instead of a feature. But I'm still happy I finished it the way it did. As it is written in ZEN FILMMAKING, "It stands on its own perfection."

2. You are right about actors, I had cast 8 major actors, and 3 of them dropped out without notice on the first day of shooting. (But thanks to Zen Filmmaking, I wasn't TOO bothered by it, since I just had to change the story around a little, and one of the attractive actresses that stayed brought a couple of her friends the fill in some of the parts and they were wonderful).

3. Many of the images turned out grainier than I had hoped, which affected the way audiences saw the film (I don't have a lot of money to buy an expensive camera, so I just used what I have, which was a small Japanese HD camera that doesn't look HD). Some of the people I showed it to didn't seem too happy with the result, and some just didn't, "Get it."

4. The crew, if they are not being paid, didn't care about the production and would frequently show up late or not at all, so much of the movie I shot by myself.

5. During editing, I would get very discouraged by the end product that I would just choose not to edit for weeks on end. Also finding music and waiting too long caused me to stagnate, and I didn't finish the edit until about 6 months later. I had to realize that I must, "Accept what I receive," and just get it done, no matter how the end product would turn out.

Overall, I must say that I had a VERY positive experience with Zen filmmaking, and I want to do it again this year. As I've said, I met a friend on the set (now a good friend) who wants to star in my next film; he's a decent actor too, IMHO.

Also, many of the actors who stuck around really enjoyed the flexibility and artistic-ness of Zen Filmmaking, saying it was one of the most fun they've ever had on a film set.

Q & A
I have a few questions for you though, if you don't mind,

1. Why did you stick to the cult-side of the film industry? (Although I love cult movies, I'm just curious).

To be honest, every time I make a really good drama, no one sees it. Films like: *The Hard Edge of Hollywood* and *Blood on the Guitar* are really, (what I considered), some of my best. But, nobody watches them. At least not in the U.S. But, movies like *Vampire Noir, Vampire Blvd., Guns of El Chupacabra, Max Hell Frog Warrior,* etc. Everybody sees 'em. So... It is just a question of supply and demand. Giving the people what they want...

2. Why was Donald G. Jackson so angry all of the time?

Like I always say used to say, *"Don is Don."* Now I say, *"Don was Don."* But, it was just who he was. He was an extremely troubled artist. As many true artists are. But, the main thing, he was always very cool to me and that is all that mattered. He was probably one of the best friends I will ever have, as he actually went out of his way to help my life in regard to the film industry. And, that is something few people, in this place we call life, actually would do.

3. *In your new book, although you've given some more specific tips on film distribution, you rarely ever talk about film festivals or film markets. What are your experiences with these, and what is some advice you would give to a budding filmmaker on distribution of a low/no budget film?*

For the most part, Film Festivals are pretty much all fixed. They are a way for the person or persons who is running them to make money. I mean, if this wasn't the case, then they would be free to enter. But, almost universally, they charge a lot of money for each film that is submitted. And, virtually none of those films are ever shown to the public.

My only advice on the Film Festival front is festivals like the *Houston* or the *Sacramento Film Festival*. In those cases, if your film is filmed in their city, then you have a much better chance of getting it shown. I have seen some films that won the *Houston Film Festival* that were just horrible beyond belief. But, because they were filmed in Houston, they won.

As detailed in my books and articles, distributors are notorious for taking your money and even if the film sells, the filmmaker never makes a dime. Why? Because the distributors lie. But, if all you want is to get it out there, you can try that route. I have known people that have not made a dime, but their film was in every video rental place on the globe.

In terms of indie distribution, I suggest going through one of the print-on-demand companies. They are free and they will get your film out there. That does not mean that people will buy your film, unless they have a reason to. For that you have to do P.R. But, it will be out there.

4. *Seriously, what do you think of film schools? (Honestly, in my opinion, I've been going to film school for 4 years here in AZ, but I've learned more from my experience actually trying to make a film than the entire time I was there).*

If you've got the money, I suggest college to everyone. Because you come out with a degree. And, at the end of the day, it doesn't matter what the degree is in, as long as you have it. But, as someone who has taught at film schools, I can tell you, (aside from me), all the professors make unrealistic promises and never really teach the reality of filmmaking. So, no matter where you go to school, if you want to be a filmmaker, you got to get out there and do it.

5. *I want to visit Hollywood this summer, is there any chance I could meet you? or Are you teaching a class in California at all or making a film? I would love to meet you or help out on one of your sets in any way.*

I've kind of stepped away from teaching right now. I'm doing a lot of other things. But, meeting me is easy. I'm always happy to sit down and have coffee. Especially if you bring a pretty girl. ☺

6. *What is your favorite film? and What is your favorite of the ones you made? (I want to buy Vampire Bikers From Hell, since the preview looked interesting. But I'd like to know which one you would prefer).*

I generally answer that my favorite film is *Blade Runner*—the studio version, not the Director's Cut. But, you probably know that because I mention it in my book, *Zen Filmmaking*. Of my films, if you want to see ideal examples of *Zen Filmmaking: Undercover X* and *Hitman City* are great examples. If you're looking for something a bit more artsy, (for lack of a better term), than *Vampire Blvd.* is a good *Zen Filmmaking* choice.

7. *Can I post info about my film, "Monique," the website, or the trailer on your site?*

I don't really have a place for that on my site. I would suggest setting up a page at MySpace and YouTube. But, your questions play really well, much like an interview. So, I will have my guy post this email on my site for a while and maybe that will send some people your direction.
Hope this helps...

All the best,
S.

ADDITIONAL QUESTION
6 June 2010

To: Dr. Shaw

I have one quick question about Zen Filmmaking that wasn't quite clear in your book. You mention that you make a shot list for your films. How do you make a shot list without a script?

Hey J,

The main thing is... Don't over think it. There are no hard and fast rules in *Zen Filmmaking*. Make it your own!

But, to answer your question, from my perspective, there are two points that may help your process:

First of all, just because there is no script, does not mean that I do not have a story idea.

Creating a Zen Film is like painting a painting: you have your canvas, your paints, and your brushes. The filmmaker is the brush. The cast is the different colors of paint. The canvas is the location. But it is the filmmaker that decides what the painting is going to look like.

What I do is to start with the story idea. Then, I decide how to best tell that story with the cast and the locations I have. At that point, I make a list of the scenes that will best tell the story within the confines of my cast and locations. That equals my shot list. Then, I go to the location and let the Zen happen. I tell the cast what the scene is about and let them play it in their own way.

But, the main thing to understand is that I never let my shot list dominate my vision. If I come up with new ideas or new situations present themselves, I always am open and ready to change and accept.

One side note here... And, I talk about this in my book Independent Filmmaking, which I know you have rear—there can only be one Captain of the Ship. You cannot let your cast and crew randomly throw in their ideas. Because this will derail your vision. You are the filmmaker, there has to be one *commander-in-chief* and if you open the process up to any and all ideas and comments, then the vision is lost.

The second process of *Zen Filmmaking* is to just let it happen while filming the process. I have done this more times than I can count but an ideal example of this is the bar scene in my film, *Undercover X*. What occurred is that my cast, cameraman, and I went into a bar. I told my cameraman to never turn off the camera, no matter what occurred. We were in and out of character, but it was all filmed. In fact, what occurred is the cameraman also became a character. I was watching the contentious relationship building between my costar and the cameraman, so I took the camera from him, told them to step into character and I filmed it. It became one of the best scenes of the movie.

The main thing is, just let it happen. Don't have any expectations. Just do it! Then, whatever comes out is perfect.

Hope this helps!!!
All the best,
S.

13 August 2010

To: Dr. Shaw

I am making another film (video) in October of this year. I have struggled for about a year trying to find a script that could fit my budget. I tried to find financing, but the entire situation was impossible. It seemed strange to me what occurred to me. I had gone to school for this kind of career path, spent a lot of my own money for the degree, yet the entire process seemed impossible for an independent filmmaker today. I am not personally struggling, though (I have a job doing something I don't like to do), but artistically I felt the filmmaking, "Zen O'clock: Time to Be," and it gave me much encouragement and insight. I read a lot of books, especially on spirituality, but this one was very wise, very small, and easy to read a few passages daily (like a daily meditation/devotional). Zen Filmmaking may be not just the best option for me right now; I feel it is the only option.

First, I'd like to say, thank you so much for your writings and inspiration. I have been interested in Zen for quite some time, but I've never taken any real steps into a meditative life. However, Zen O'clock had somewhat of a profound effect on how I viewed life...so thank you.

Second, I have a question for you, more of a personal question if you don't mind: How did you grow up? I read you went to high school in Hollywood, but what kind of person were you, and how did you come to have a wise view of life or I guess how did you become a Zen Buddhist?

Third, in, "Zen Filmmaking," (the book) when asked in an interview why you shoot on video you said, "...As soon as Cameron or Lucas does something on video then it will all of the sudden be the cool thing to do and then all of the major film companies will say they knew it all along" (p.168). I was amazed when I read this because this was 1993, and now it has become true. What do you see in future of movies?

Sincerely,
J.

Hey J,

Always good to hear from you. Glad you like *Zen O'clock*.

To answer your question(s):

Second, I have a question for you, more of a personal question if you don't mind: How did you grow up? I read you went to high school in Hollywood, but what kind of person were you, and how did you come to have a wise view of life or I guess how did you become a Zen Buddhist?

From my earliest memories forward, I was drawn to Eastern Thought. So, karma, destiny, my past life, I don't know... But, it has always been who I am.

Third, in, "Zen Filmmaking," (the book) when asked in an interview why you shoot on video you said, "...As soon as Cameron or Lucas does something on video then it will all of the sudden be the cool thing to do and then all of the major film companies will say they knew it all along" (p.168). I was amazed when I read this because this was 1993, and now it has become true. What do you see in future of movies?

In many ways, it is anybody's guess. But, with the rapidly advancing digital and electronic technologies I think we are quickly moving away from physical things like DVDs, Blu-Rays and the like. I mean, think about it, just a couple of years ago you couldn't watch movies on your computer, or on your TV via the Internet. Now, it is rapidly moving to being the only way you watch a movie. But, we will still need films to watch. So, that is where young filmmakers like yourself come in. KEEP MAKING MOVIES !!!!

All the best,
S.

9 September 2010

To: Dr. Shaw

I am in the middle of casting my new film Alan's Day, a psychological thriller about a soldier battling hallucinations and Russian spies. I was surprised that as I went out to meet people and audition them how interested in Zen Filmmaking they were. They were thrilled that the movie did not have a script, and I did not force them into a huge time commitment. After explaining what Zen filmmaking is all about and how it frees the artist from the constraints of expectation and desire, usually found in the traditional filmmaking process, most people, "Get it," yet I have had a few people who did not get it and actually became hostile to both myself and my casting director. There were at least four different people, who we had spoken to during the course of our pre-production adventure who would say negative things like: "You can't make a 'real' movie without a script," or when a local film director, who had heard about my project, e-mailed the lead actor who I had casted and was trying to convince him to leave my project. He was saying that, "Zen Filmmaking is a load of crap," and so on and so forth. I don't know how to respond to these people, or what to do when they tell the people that I have on cast and crew that what I am trying to do is nonsense. So far, I have had the most fun making a movie by the Zen method, and I feel that it actually makes one even more skilled and focused when it comes to the art of filmmaking (like the skill and focus it takes to be a champion archer, or pianist, etc.). But these people really make it hard on us who are trying to make this movie in the most positive and creative way we can. Have you ever experienced detractors, people who just did not get what you were trying to do and tried to make it hard? And if so, how did you deal with people like this, so that your project could go smoothly?

Hey J,

As I am sure you have realized, most actors are very nice when you talk about *Zen Filmmaking*. They either get it or they don't. If they don't get it, they just move on. If they do get it, they become a great part of your team. But, we all meet our detractors. There are always those negative people out there who want to bring you and your project down for no good reason but their ego or whatever??? I certainly have had mine. The stories I could tell you... But, there is no point in confrontation. It equals nothing. The best defense is success with your project. And success is getting it done. So, that is all you should focus on. If someone is calling your cast and they believe what they hear, maybe they weren't right for you film. Just trust the process. Trust your feelings and make your movie.

All the best,
S.

29 October 2010
To: Dr. Shaw

Your books have really opened the door to reality for me. It may seem obsessive, but still again I thank you for your work. A lot of filmmaking books I've read did not prepare me for some of the real things that go on while shooting a film, or they would require me to raise a certain amount of money that I know I would not be able to raise to get a film completed. Last week, I was filming my second attempt at feature film, Alan's Day. This time around, I did not write a script but wanted to trust my intuition as a guiding force. Well, the production came out better than I expected. One particular actor, though, did not feel comfortable without a script. She kept on making it more difficult than it was when she was talking to me about her character, etc. before her day of shooting.

So, I wrote a short script for the day and gave it to her and the other actor who was accompanying her. Well, when the shooting day came, everyone acted as if they never read the script. They still didn't know what was going on. So, I tried to break it down, step by step, but then, their performances became boring and wooden. So, then I just said, "Ok, let's just play with it, and see what happens." I wrote some notes down, and allowed them to improv a little based on my notes. Then, everything became much more natural and interesting as I directed them without the script. This is just one of the few examples during the past week that a light bulb went off in my head and I thought, "Yep, Scott Shaw was right."

Anyways, I was wondering what do you do about crewmembers? I have had a wonderful time with the cast. Besides a few small ego issues, which dissipate quickly with cast, I never have had a big problem with actors. But on my set last week, I hired on a boom operator/sound mixer and 2 make-up artists. They both seemed very open and nice when I met them prior to shooting. But starting on the first day of filming, we had problems. The boom operator was following us to the third location and got lost. He left me a message on my phone telling me he won't be working on the project anymore. So, I was left to handle sound myself. Then the make-up artist lost a small make-up kit while filming and demanded that I pay her compensation for it (well-over the original cost). I didn't even want the make-up artists in the first place, but it was a suggestion from my lead actor. So, I felt really bad that I didn't put my foot down hard enough on this, since I ended up owing her a lot of money.

Have you dealt with crew like this? What do you do?

From: J.

Hey J,

I'm smiling, because what you went through happens all the time. And, I don't know if there is any way around it. I've seen it on both high budget sets, where people walk off, and, of course, on low budget sets where people decide they are just too good for the project. All I can say is that you just have to adapt and go with the flow...

The only advice I can give you, if you want to call it that, is that small is large. The less crew you have to deal with the better. The less cast, the better.

On a case-by-case basis: makeup people are notorious for trying to snake money out of you. On most of my movies, I don't use 'em. *Roller Blade Seven, Guns of El Chupacabra, Samurai Vampire Bikers from Hell, Undercover X, Hard Edge of Hollywood,* etc., etc., etc... No makeup. The MUA's are just too much trouble. If I do use a MUA, I make sure that the really want to be on the set and to do it for the sake of credit.

Re: actors who want scripts. *"You're fired!"* Never-never bow down to the demands of actors. If they want to be in your project, great!!! But, make them do it your way, (whatever your way is). The minute you start giving into their demands everything becomes convoluted.

In my case, I have my, (very minimal), shot list for what I hope to shoot in a day. And, I never show it to an actor. If they are a real actor, they don't need to know what's coming next. They just need to be ready to do it.

Funny story... When I was shooting *Vampire Abstracta* last year, I was sitting on a couch getting ready to do a scene with my lead actress and I was glancing at my shot list. She was leaning on my shoulder and got to read it. She got so excited, *"I feel so special, I got to see Scott Shaw's shot list."* It needs to be like that. Hire people that really want to be in a film and are not going to give you grief, making you play by their rules. Because, at the end of the day, it is you who is providing them with the opportunity to be in a film.

Hope your project goes great!!!

All the best,
S.

30 March 2011
To: Dr. Shaw

Hello, this is J. Since we had last spoke, I was in the middle of shooting my film Alan's Day. A lot of the footage I liked, but it was hard to put it together, and I almost dropped the whole thing. It is still not edited. So, I put together another production, a vampire film called, "Draugierre," (the trailer is here on YouTube), this past February.

Now, I was trying your 'two-day' feature as a challenge, and I must say, it ALMOST worked. Everything was going good up until the last four hours of the second day of filming. What happened was, I lost my lens mid-way through production. But, I had a back-up camera, and although it was a smaller consumer-looking camera, the actors acted really funny when I pulled it out. It was like they didn't want to do anything because they thought I was 'cheating' the production by using a 'cheaper' camera (even though the camera was HD and I knew it was going to work well the other footage). The actors pretty much bailed on me at the end, expecting to come back. But now they are all busy and make excuses every time I call them back for another shoot. We were so close, yet it seemed like all of the sudden they didn't believe in me anymore and just walked off.

In your book, "Independent Filmmaking: Secrets of the Craft," you talked a little bit about production shutdown. But I've never had a situation where the actors just kind of let go, just because of damn camera. I, mean, (and sorry for my frustration), what do they expect? I must have told them a hundred times that my films are not Hollywood movies, and they aren't supposed to be! Have you ever encountered a situation like this? I'm just curious to see how you would have handled it. I'm tempted, really, to just edit what I have and move on to another film and get it right. I just didn't expect the actor's expectations to be so high.

This also leads me to another question, and it is about editing. What's your philosophy when it comes to editing? I've seen Roller Blade Seven and Hitman City, (both of which I liked), but both films seemed very different in their editing approach. That was another thing, I was wondering about, since both of your books didn't seem to delve very far with editing.

Anyway, Zen Filmmaking, and I wish more of my peers would understand, works! Thank you for your writings. I guess maybe it is more of a stepping-stone process that gets better the more you practice.

Sincerely, J.

Hey J,

Always good to hear from you...

Cast members walk, my friend. That's why I never use scripts. *Fuck 'em.* What's the line in that old Thin Lizzy song? *"If that chick don't want to know then forget her."*

This is also why, as time has gone on, I have used smaller and smaller casts; people I can trust. But, sometimes that doesn't always work either. In the movie that I released with the title, *The Canceled Movie,* you can see the whole process, where two of the actresses were just bad, with bad attitudes, and I pulled the plug at the end of the first day.

Though I initially thought the movie was just a wash, after a month or two I got to thinking... *"Wait a minute. I think I do have a movie here."* And, I did...

The thing that I recommend that you do is to finish your movie. If you have to tie your story together with a few new cast members, do it. If you have to add some narration and not film any more, that is even easier. But, by finishing it, you are showing the people that walked that you don't need them. Because no actor is more important than the completed film!

In terms of editing, *"Just do it!"* Remove yourself from all of the traditional editing protocol and expectation you may have. Just let it happen.

If the move is two hours, all good. If it is one hour, fine. If it is twenty minutes, that is great too. Just get it done.

As you probably know, I am anti-story. As I say, *"The stories have all been told."* So, don't define your project or your edit by telling a perfect story. Just be natural, let it happen. Let one scene flow to the next. If it doesn't make perfect sense, that's fine. That just becomes the style of that movie.

As for me, I always change; I always use new editing styles. My latest film, *Count Vlogula,* takes editing in a completely different direction than I have ever used before. So, my advice is just be free and let the cinematic art happen.
Hope this helps...

S.

Talkin' Collobration

Hello Mr. Shaw,

I love your films, my favorite one is Shotgun Blvd. I'm a fourteen-year-old filmmaker myself and I love your Zen style of filmmaking. If you are ever in New York City, where I live, it would be such an honor to make/direct a Zen short film of some sort with you. Thank you!

Your fan, D.

Hey D.,

And, PLEASE, call me Scott !!!

Great to hear you are a filmmaker. You are really lucky to live in NYC. It is such a great place to make films. So many cool backdrops.

It's been a few years since I was there. But, I would be more than happy to do a film together next time I get to the Eastside...

All the best,
S.

Hello Scott,

Thank you so much for replying! It's an honor to talk to a professional filmmaker such as yourself! I actually had an idea for a collaboration where you shot some Zen scenes of your own where you live, and then I added new scenes to it using my actors, and maybe linking the two stories together through some sort of phone call or something. I know you are probably a very busy man; I feel privileged just to get a message from you at all. If you like how it sounds then that's great, and if you don't that's ok too, I'm just really happy I got a message back from one of my filmmaking idols! Another idea was that if you have any unused footage from previous footage or unfinished films I could film scenes with my actors and finish it up. Again, just a crazy idea of mine, if you don't like the idea that's fine. I have one question: How did you do the "Rollercam" in movies like The Roller Blade Seven? I'm in love with those shots where the camera speeds right towards the actors and want to know how to do something like that myself. Ok, this message has gone on too long, sorry to bug you.

Your fan, D.

Hey D.,

    Your collaboration idea is a very good one. I have known a few people who have done similar things and the results are always very interesting. I'm kind of in a weird position however where I can't really do something like that because of who owns the rights, who can valid the performer releases, etc., etc... It all gets very complicated. But, thanks for asking.

    Regarding your question about RB7 and the rollercam. We just had a guy who was a really great roller skater. We gave him a Bolex with a wide-angle lens, told him what to capture and then used the best of what he filmed. Hope that helps.

Keep making movies!!!

S.

Ok, thanks for replying about the idea. I really like the rollercam, and even though I don't have a Bolex I'm getting a Canon Rebel t2i pretty soon, and there's probably someone at my school who's a good roller skater. I know there's a lot of skateboarders, hopefully something like that would achieve a similar effect.

Film Scoring

Hello there!

Thank you for being willing to answer my question! I'm actually asking for my friend. He's trying to get some connections going in film. He wants to get into scoring for films, he's a producer/dj/musician and recently moved from England. He asked me if I knew anyone so I told him i would ask around.

Getting into film scoring is a bit tricky and very easy at the same time. If he wants to make money immediately, it is a bit harder to get that first foot in the door. If he is willing to do it for free, to get some screen credits, it is much easier. The quickest way to do it, on either level, is to check what films are currently in pre-production in the Trades: *Hollywood Reporter* and *Variety* and even at places like *Craig's List* and on casting websites like *Actors Access, Now Casting,* and *L.A. Casting.* Then, contact the producer of the film and see if they need someone to score the movie. It is always easiest if he approaches the producer as early into pre-production as possible that way he may also share in any PR that the film takes on before it is completed.

The low budget indies are always easier to get that first job but they rarely pay.

Hope this helps in some small way.

All the best,
S.

Talkin' Distribution

I'm trying to find a distributor for this movie that will give some sort of advance and it's so hard – even though there's a bankable actor in the film no one wants something this offbeat!

Yeah... Getting distribution is a tricky deal. I don't know anybody who is giving advances anymore. I know a guy who did a movie with Bruce Campbell, and he can't even get an advance. Mostly, what distributors do is take your movie, make money on it, and then either lie and tell you that they made nothing or charge you for their services. It's a crazy market now. I understand your friend Lloyd (Kaufman) takes movies and distributes them but doesn't pay. So, it's just one of those things... What is it worth to you to get your movie out there, possibly seen, and hope it will lead to something else ???

Yeah, I'm screening it in two weeks! I'm hoping if I don't make an advance i can get a smaller company to take it and work out a very specific contract with them to where they HAVE to push it, and give me a cut.

Hey Scott,
I'm thinking of self-distributing my new movie like i have my two previous films as the distributor I've been talking to doesn't get back to me as much as I'd like and I'm not loving the distribution deal they offered me. my two previous films were not very successful, but this one has gotten more attention from the press so I'm

thinking controlling everything about its distribution is the way to go. i might even run some facebook ads for it. as someone who i imagine has had success in self-distribution would you recommend this?

By the way: This question is kind of long, so I understand if you're too busy to answer it, I thank you for all the advice you've given me so far and it's really helped me.

No problem D.
    Always happy to help.
    Your question is a bit complicated as you have to decide the market you are aiming for. The fact is, (as you know), a lot of people have made a lot of movies, and I've known many people who have had very big stars in their indie, (that cost a lot of money to get), but even with this their sales were very low. Then you look at a film like the original Blair Witch that did pretty well. They claim this was all due to internet marking but that is not true. But, what their internet marking campaign did do was to find them someone who gave them money to make it bigger and better and then get it out there into the public eye, which made it look like it was an indie that was so great that everyone must see it. The fact is, Facebook marketing only hits a very specific group of people and it is expensive—which is great if that is what you want. A bit better way for movie PR is to set up an actual website for the film that the search engines will find and then you guide people to that through Facebook or whatever. On that site you have Production Still, cast and crew

interviews, and all that kind of PR which you seem very good at.

On that site, what you are doing is making your film look like it must be a must see.

As your films have had screenings, have had articles written about them, and should be available through *Amazon* via *CreateSpace,* they are out there enough to have a Wikipedia page, which you should make and put a link to your website. Now, I am no fan of Wikipedia as it is inhabited by a bunch of people with nothing better to do with their life. But, this will get you notoriety, leading to free PR, leading to sales—hopefully... You may have to fight the meaningless Wikipedia hordes to keep it up there at first but by doing this you can have forever publicity for your film.

The fact is, there is no absolute formula anymore, especially for the less than mainstreams films that people like you or I make. But, those are a few ideas that seem to work.

One way or the other good luck.

S.

Thank you so much for the advice, Scott!! I'll definitely start working on Wikipedia pages and such, I always appreciate your honesty.

SECTION III:
Zen Filmmaking: The Techniques

Acting for the Camera

Unless you are creating non-narrative films, like I have been focusing on for the past few years, acting is at the heart of any film. It is the actor who gets your story told. But actors are also, many times, the thing that makes a film hard to watch; as they are the central focus, their performances are the first thing that is commonly judged about a film.

Acting has evolved over the years. If you like to watch older films from the 1930s and 1940s like I do, you will immediately notice that the acting was much bigger back then. The performances where much more exaggerated. This is due to the fact that most of the actors of that era were schooled on the stage. In the theatre their performances needed to be bigger. From this, they took this same acting style with them to the silver screen.

This is one of the reasons that I so much like working with my friend Conrad Brooks. He came from that era and he acts like he is still in that era. I love his performances.

In independent filmmaking, particularly the low to no budget genre, acting is what generally makes a film watchable or not. Now, this is a doubled edged sword because most people working at this level of the film industry are inexperienced actors—at least in terms of on-camera experience. If a person can remain natural in their performance, then there is no problem. But, most people can't. Most people, at least the inexperienced, when they act, they are acting.

And, this is what may kill the believability of their performance.

Also, particularly when people are attempting to make a spoof film, they intentionally overact. They believe this is how it was done. But, in actually, this is not the case. Bad acting is just that; bad acting. It is a whole onto itself. Therefore, by attempting to recreate it, defeats the entire purpose.

Now, there have been some great performances based upon spoofing an actor or an acting era. Billy Zane did a great job in the last of the Ed Wood scripts, *I Woke Up Early the Day I Died*. This film had no dialogue, but the performances were great. And, of course, the spoof-based performances of talented actors like Johnny Depp have been great. But, these are very intentional performances given by highly talented actors. When one is inexperienced and doing this, it does not translate well to the screen.

If we look to the Republic Serial from the 1930s, 1940s, on into the 1950s, there was some great programing made in that era—whether it was for TV or the big screen. Series like *Commando Cody* and *The Adventures of Fu Manchu* truly defined an era and were the first to bring comic book type heroes to the screen. If we watch the acting in these serials, it was over the top. But, it was over the top, specific to that era. Just as when we watch Capt. James T. Kirk, (William Shatner), on the original *Star Trek* series, his acting is over the top but believable in its era.

To try to emulate these performances never really translates well to screen. I know, because we did this in *Roller Blade Seven*. Though the style of acting we employed did set the stage for the overall vibe of the film, most people didn't get it and did not understand the influences we were harkening back to, as times had changed and most who watched the RB7 film(s) were not aware of that era gone past or were not yet even born when it took place.

To this end, and through the years upon years I have been making films, I find it is far better to simply be natural in all onscreen performances—natural to your era. Even if your film is a spoof, by being true to yourself, by being who you are on screen, while wrapped in the cloak of a character, the audience will find your performance far more enjoyable to watch than if you try to be something you are not and perform as those people did in times gone past.

Working with the Actor

At the heart of any film is the actor. They are the ones who portray the filmmaker's vision and relay the characters to the audience. Though the actor is the most essential part in the depiction of any story, they are also the element that can make or break a film's production. As such, a filmmaker must be very conscious in who they cast for their film.

With this understanding as a basis, from a personal perspective, I do not believe any actor who has worked with me or has been in one of my films would have anything bad to say about me. In fact, I have never personally had any bad interactions with actors on my sets. Why? Because I cast my films very consciously.

Most actors, whether they are extremely famous or new to the game are very nice people. They are actors, so they are happy to be a part of a film.

There are commonly two levels of actors you work with on the independent film level: the name actors and the novice actors. The name actors you cast for the marketability of their name and their expertise in the craft. The novice actors you cast, most commonly, due to the lack of a high enough budget to afford a cast full of experienced actors.

This beginning stated, the fact of the matter is, on an independent film set, you are more likely to have a problem with a novice actor, than an established one. This is because the established actor understands the process. The newbies do not. Thus, they come onto any set, even a low-budget set, with many expectations.

I have personally worked with very famous actors. When they came on my set and saw only the most minimal of crew and equipment, they did not blink an eye for they understood all that matters is the finished product. And, they knew that is what I could and would supply, a competent finished product.

On the other hand, I have had a few experiences when newbie actors would come onto my set and state, *"I expected more."* But, on the independent level, "More," is generally not what you have to offer. It is for this reason that I believe one of the most important things you can do in your casting process is to tell your actors what to expect. Don't exaggerate, don't lie, just tell them the truth. This will help you overcome many potential problems before they begin. If a new actor is expecting a major production, it is best to let them hold out until they are perhaps cast in one sometime in the future.

I have found time-and-time again when a person is new to Hollywood, they expect to be a famous superstar overnight. Though I wish them all the best, for most of them, this will not occur. What I always explain to them is that what I have to offer them is a stepping-stone in their career— a film to be in where they gain on-camera experience and will actually have scenes in a film to show their family, friends, and potential agents. Plus, they will be a part of a film that is actually released on DVD and/or by other means that they are actually in. This provides a lot of credibility to an actor.

The main point here is that you must cast

your film consciously and honestly. You must bring in people who want to work with you at whatever level you are working at. From this, the filmmaking process will be as pain free as possible and who knows, you may emerge with the next big indie film.

Understanding Improv Acting

If you ask me, *"What do I think about improvisational acting?"* I will tell you that I believe it is the ultimate level of human performance both on stage and in front of the camera. But, I will also say that there are very few actors who do it well.

Acting is a craft. It is a developed craft. To act naturally, especially in front of the camera or an audience, is not easy. It takes practice.

It is for this reason that people go to acting classes—which, as I have long stated, are total bullshit. Acting classes are simply a way for a teacher to make money and for the students to believe that they have a chance of breaking into the film industry. They are wrong. Acting classes are not the ticket.

Why? Because acting classes are not acting. And, though improv techniques are often taught in acting classes, those performances never equal anything. They are just mental masturbation in front of classmates. They don't cost anything, and they certainly do not cut into a film's budget when the performances are bad and have to be reshot or cut out of a film altogether.

The fact of the matter is, improv acting is a very subtle art form. Many actors think it is simply about talking. It is not. Improv acting is also about listening.

Due to the fact that most people believe that improv acting is about talking, that is all they do. You take novice actors, put them together and ask them to improv, what you will more than likely see is two people attempting to talk over one another and take control of the scene. The more actors you put together, the more convoluted the scene becomes.

All this being stated, when I created *Zen Filmmaking*, improv was one of the key components to its actualization. But, the improv I have used in my Zen Films is very controlled.

What this means is that, if I know a person can actually believably improv, I tell them what the scene is about and then I let them run with it. If the storyline needs any correction, I stop them, redirect their dialogue, and allow them to recommence. But, if I see that an actor cannot move the story forward in a natural manner, what I do is feed them their lines.

Due to the fact of *Zen Filmmaking*, many people falsely believe that movies like *The Roller Blade Seven* and *Max Hell Frog Warrior* were improv'd. This is not the case. For the most part, in those films, actors, including a few of the noted (famous) ones, were feed their lines. The great exception to this is when Joe Estevez and Donald G. Jackson go head-to-head in *The Return of the Roller Blade Seven* and dish out a twenty minute scene; uncut—all improved. It's awesome!

The essence is that improv is an actor being natural in any given situation. It is about the actor presenting the story, through words, movements, and actions, in the most natural matter possible. This is the whole reason I do not use scripts in my films. Many actors, even in high-budget performances, become very unnatural when speaking memorized words. I think we have all seen movies and TV shows where it is obvious, the actor is acting. But, by removing a much structure as possible, than a performance becomes more natural.

But... And, this is a BIG but... An actor must possess the ability to silence their own mind if they hope to improve with any believability. They must become the character they are portraying. And, this is the point where most actors fail at improv. They base their words and their actions upon ego. Of how they want their character to be perceived and how they wish to drive the story of their character forward.

Sure, if a charter is created around an actor's own personality, then they can play it fine. But, move them away from themselves, and this is where the problems arrive.

True improv comes from a very Zen, selfless state. A good improv actor is one who can remove themselves from the equation and simple BE.

This is hard, as acting is based in ego. A movie or a play is inhabited by a group of people who believe that they have something to offer—that they are special and good enough to be ACTORS.

Think about it. If you ask the average person if they would like to be in a film, they would, *"No way. I can't do that!"* The actor on the other hand is all about themselves and their believed, unique specialness. "I'm great! I should be famous."

Therefore, the ultimate truth about improv acting if that for it to be successfully accomplished, the actor must be able to put themselves and their ego aside and simple BE in the moment. They must allow the character to be the character. They must let themselves go and naturally step into who and what that character is. From this, true improv acting is embraced.

Film Making Verses Video Making

Ever since the dawning of the video age of filmmaking, in the late 1980s and early 1990s, the face of filmmaking has changed. In fact, I guess I was a part of that revolution in that I helped to usher it along with my movie, *Samurai Vampire Bikers from Hell;* which was one of the first films, shot on video, to gain international distribution and to be shown in theaters. This being stated, there is large difference between filmmaking and video making. And, this is a fact that is lost to many of the new breed of video filmmakers.

In what has evolved into the digital age of video filmmaking, all anyone needs is a few dollars to buy and cheap video camera, a few dollars to buy some video tape, and a few more dollar to get a video editing program for their computer, and they can make a movie. As someone who was at the forefront of speaking about and teaching this technology, I think this is great. It allows people to be creative for a small amount of money. But, is it actual, *"Film Making?"* No, it is not. I know because I work on both film and video.

Something that many/most of the new breed of video filmmakers do not understand, as they never learned true filmmaking, is that the, *"Film,"* making process is very complicated and extremely expensive. For example, with a video camera, all you do is throw in the videotape. With film, first you must understand the differences between the various types of films, their ASA rating, and the appropriate amount of footage you must buy to load into your specific type of film magazine. Then, and most importantly, you must know how to load your camera—as each and every film camera loads differently. An Aaton loads differently from an Arri. An Éclair loads differently than a Beaulieu. A Bolex loads differently than a Panavision, and so on. To be a true filmmaker, a true cinematography, you must possess this knowledge before you can even begin to shoot your movie. And, this is just the first step...

In filmmaking schools, and I know because I teach at them; one of the main prerequisites is classes in still photography—using film-based cameras. Why? Because film is very different from video. The way it is lighted, the way it works with its central subject, its depth of field, and so on. It is understood that for any filmmaker to actually make a film, they must have photography, with film, as a basis.

In time, this may change. But, as the majority of the high-production movies and televisions shows are still shot on film, this will not change for some time.

And, this is just the beginning. With a video camera, you have whatever lens is on your camera to work with, and that is that. In filmmaking, with film cameras, you must understand the various lenses, what they do, how they focus, how they frame a subject, and how to set the exposure on them.

Then there's the audio... On a video camera all you have to do is plug in a microphone. For film, you have to have an off-board deck that can run at the same speed as your camera and somebody who knows how to operate it.

It terms of the post-production of film, this is also very complicated and very expensive. You must first have your film developed. Then you must sync your film and audio tapes. Then, depending on how you plan to edit your movie, you must either transfer the film to Work Prints so you do not damage your original footage, or you must telecine it and transfer it to Beta Masters so it can be acquired into an Avid or whatever other type of editing system you are using. Then, you must produce either a final Answer Print or a final Beta Master; depending on what is your deliver requirements.

So, for you video makers out there, who think that you are actually filmmakers, think again. You are moviemakers, not filmmakers. Your project may be good, it may be bad, but it has nothing to do with, *"Film Making."* It is for this reason that many of the aficionados of the craft refuse to work on video.

These are important facts to keep in mind when you define yourself and your project...

DSLR Cinematography

Over the past several years many people have taken to using their DSLR cameras to film their independent films and music videos. The reason for this is twofold: One, the cameras are generally much cheaper to buy than a good camera that is actually designed to shoot live action video. Two, due to the fact that you can easily change the lenses on these cameras they give the would-be filmmaker varying cinematic options. Though, on a basic level, these cameras do provide a fairly good video image, there are also several problems with using them as a tool to film a competent movie.

The initial problem that arises with using a DSLR, as a filmmaking tool, comes from the way in which it focuses. Whereas the focusing mechanism on a video camera is designed to find, focus, and capture a moving image, this is not the case with a DSLR. DSLR focusing is designed to capture a still image, (as they are actually designed as a still frame camera). To this end, if you are going to use your DSLR camera to film a movie you really need to work with lock-off shots. Meaning, set up a tripod, get your actors in place, and then let them do their stuff with little or no spherical or to-and-fro movement. If you work within a standardized lock-off shot format, then your DSLR can capture a nice image.

For me, personally, I find the lock-off shot very boring. I like visual movement. To this end, whenever I use one of my DSLR cameras to film people, I very precisely lock the focus and keep the subject(s) at a static and standardized distance. From this, the figures appear to have movement while keeping them in focus and preventing the camera from attempting to find focus.

The second problem with using a DSLR camera, as a filmmaking tool, comes from its capability to record sound. Almost every digital camera from the point and shoots up to the high end DSLRs now have built-in microphones. The problem is, these microphones are terrible. They produce horrible sound. In controlled internal situations you can get okay audio, but never good. If you go outside, forget about it.

Most higher-end DSLRs do have an external microphone input. If you are going to shoot with a DSLR get a high-end mic and use it! This being said, the way a DSLR processes sound is also not as good as the way a camera designed to shoot video does.

Now, I'm not going to go into a long discourse about sound here. If you want to read the all and the everything about the superiority of the XLR microphones and the appropriate microphones and cables that drive them you can read my book, *Zen Filmmaking* or find information online. I will say, high-end mics are not designed to be feed into a camera through a mini plug, as the DSLR provides. Your sound will be altered. It will be much better than using the on-board mic, but it will be altered. So, expect that.

On the other side of the issue there are some microphones that are designed to mount on a DSLR camera and provide you with superior sound. Yes, they do give you better sound. But again, they are not a professional XLR microphone, driven through an XLR port, so you must keep that in mind.

Personally, whenever I use a DSLR, as a filmmaking tool, I use it only to capture a visual image. I never expect the sound to be usable.

The fact is, the DSLR is, no doubt, going to continue to be used in filmmaking situations. But, if you use one, you must keep in mind that though they can capture video that is not what they are designed to do. It is an afterthought. If you plan to shoot a visually stimulating film, the best thing to do is to actually go with a camera that is designed to shoot video. The best cameras for that purpose have always been the ones created by Sony. Though Canon is a big player in the market, their cameras forever have underlying issues. Sony is a much better product.

At the end of the day, if you want to be a filmmaker, I always say, get out there and do it. Make your movie in the best way (any-way) you can. So, if you have a DSLR to work with, do it. Even if you just have a point and shoot or your phone—if you want to film visual images, use whatever you have.

This being said, it is important to keep in mind that every medium has its limitations. Work with what you have but understand the limitations.

Filmmaking and Urban Realism

Though I, of course, follow the *Zen Filmmaking* concept in my filmmaking practices; what I also practice is what I call, *Urban Realism.*

Urban Realism is using whatever environment you have at your disposal to make your movie. What this means is that I do not alter my situation or locations. Instead, I simply embrace them. Whereas most filmmakers construct their sets, what I do is to simply use whatever sets or locations I have available to me and integrate them into my films.

With *Urban Realism* instead of constructing locations, you go out and find locations that best portray the story you are trying to convey.

A few good examples in some of my films have been the ranch we used when we filmed *Guns of El Chupacabra.* We did not bring in all of those old worn-out industrial dump trucks, bulldozers, and the like. They were already there. We simply added them to the landscape of the film. Another good example is in *Undercover X, Samurai Johnny Frankenstein,* and *Hitman City,* we filmed at the Los Angeles Union Station. This is an old train station with an Art Nouveau style of architecture. By filming in this location not only did this add a great visual backdrop to the film, but it also provided scope to the film by having the patrons as a human backstory. In *Undercover X* we also used the subway in Tokyo. Another very visual location which provided human depth to the film. And, these are just a couple of examples.

If you study my films, you can see many-many more.

On the more basic level, I have used one of my actor's living rooms several times in my films. He has a great interior design; the kind that everyone who contacts me about the location assumes that it is a set that was actually constructed. It was not. It is simply designed by the actor with his choice of posters, wall hangings, furniture, and the like.

In terms of production value, *Urban Realism* truly adds scope to your film. In terms of budget, for the indie filmmaker, it provides your film with visually interesting locations without the costs associated with renting or creating them.

So, whether you're filming in your own downtown area, or at bridges or fields that you live closely to, by utilizing *Urban Realism* and taking your production to these locations, you make your film much larger and more visually interesting.

Do Something Every Day

Everybody who wants to make a movie wants to make a movie. They will think, plan, dream, and talk about making it. They may write and rewrite a script. But, few will every put anything to film. This is a mistake, for it is the person who wants to make a movie and then makes that movie that is the one who has truly accomplished something.

As I state over and over again, *"Making a movie is not easy."* But, even creating the cheapest and the worst film in the world is better than making no film at all if filmmaking is your desire. Yet, few people follow this path. As stated, the prefer to think and talk about making a film rather than actually making it. Why? Because thinking, talking, and dreaming is much easier than actually doing what it takes to get it done.

People who desire to make a film also, often, learn none of the skills that it takes to actually make a film. They see themselves as the creative force and, as such, they believe that when the time is right then they will be able to hire or bring in the people to shoot the camera, do the sound, put on the makeup, light the set, and do all of the etcetera that goes *hand-in-hand* with filmmaking. Again, this is the wrong ideology to possess if you hope to be a filmmaker—especially a filmmaker on the independent level.

You need to know what you're doing. You need to know how get things, everything, done if you truly hope to get your film made. You need to know how to do everything on your set, leaving it no other person if it comes to that.

How do you do this? You do it. You practice. You try. You keep trying until you know how to DO.

For any new filmmaker, my suggestion is, *you do something every day.* With today's technology you no longer need to carry around large, expensive camera equipment. All you need is a DSLR camera, a *point-and-shoot* camera, or even your smart phone. Pretty much everyone has one of these. Then, get out there and start to learn how to make your movie. Shoot footage every day. It does not have to be a scripted film. If you want it to be, sure, do that. But, if not, simply film images. Learn how to capture images in the way you desire them to be captured. Once you have captured a suitable amount put them together in a small presentation.

There! Then! You have accomplished something! You have created something; a film. You are a filmmaker and not just someone who sits around and dreams and talk about making a film. From this point, the sky is the limit.

SECTION IV:
The Zen Films

Would Your Ever Make Another Roller Blade Seven?

"Would you ever make another Roller Blade Seven?" I get asked this question fairly frequently. In fact, as RB7 was just named number twenty-seven of, *"The One-Hundred Best B-Movies of All Time,"* at *Pulse Magazine,* (thanks guys), I have been asked that question several times this week. Last year the question was asked a lot when I was named number ten on the list, *The Best Movie Trash Creators* on imdb.com.

To answer, *"Yes, I would."* In fact, I would love to make another film of that caliber. The problem is, what we did then for relatively little money would be very-very expensive to do today.

Don Jackson and I made *Roller Blade Seven* and *Return of the Roller Blade Seven* for about thirty-thousand dollars. We shot it on 16mm and doing that, in itself, is not cheap. During the production, our executive producer had us add extra, *"Name Talent,"* which wasn't in the original deal. We had set the Name Talent standard at two: Don Stroud and William Smith. But, she kept getting new ideas, so the money went out: Karen Black (RIP) was $3,000.00 and Frank Stallone was $6,000.00. Now, I was happy to work with both of these people, as they are both very talented actor, but they did cost money.

More than that though, when we made RB7 it was a different time in the film industry. People wanted to be a part of something. So, virtually every person who was in the film, including myself, was paid no money for his or her participation. But, they were happy to do it. I mean if you look at some of the scenes, there were upwards of over fifty people in one shot. They were all great and very nice people.

Also, we shot RB7 with no filming permits. We would simply go to the locations we had picked and film.

It was a different time. You could do things like that. At one point, when we were shooting out in the desert, a sheriff's helicopter landed to check us out. As long as we had no guns, which we didn't, they were all good. They flew off and filming continued...

Since 911, everything has gotten sketchy. It is much harder, if not impossible, to shoot with that many people without getting filming permits, renting the location, and all that entails... Hell, it's hard to shoot with even a couple of people nowadays. Which means, it would cost a lot of money to bring a film like RB7 up again

Now, RB7 was not without its problems. Though I wrote a long chapter about the production of the film in my book, *Zen Filmmaking,* I plan to write another article, *"Roller Blade Seven: Darkness in the Light,"* on the subject about all the negative and bad things that took place during filming and post production; including the fact, I was totally broke by the end of the production, so much so that I had to sell my *1934 D'Angelico New Yorker,* just to survive. A guitar I have never been able to replace. And, that's just one story... A lot of shit went down.

But... All this being said, people still watch and talk about the film and that is great! Many hate it. Calling it one of the worst films ever made. Maybe... But, many also like it. They love the bizarre, psychedelic, abstract nature of the first Zen Film.

In closing, I would love to do another *Roller Blade Seven*. In fact, Don and I planned to do the next chapter as, *Wheelzone Rangers*. But, we got distracted and made other films; both individually and as a team and never got back to doing it. Then, he passed away and all that is left of the *Zen Filmmaking* team is me.

All this being said, if someone out there has the money, (I know I don't), and would like to finance another bizarre wild ride into the *Wheelzone,* give me a call. I am willing and I am available. ☺

What Happened to the Sword?

I have recently been receiving a bunch of questions about what happened to the samurai sword I used in *The Roller Blade Seven* and do I still have it? In fact, one person offered to buy it from me for quite a substantial amount of money.

Actually, I used that same sword in a few samurai based movies I did back in the early 1990s: *Samurai Vampire Bikers from Hell,* (a minor shot in) *Samurai Johnny Frankenstein,* and in *Samurai Ballet.* Then, I put it to rest for a long-long time. I used a different sword in *Max Hell Frog Warrior* and *Guns of El Chupacaba.*

By my nature, I am not a collector of THINGS. In fact, I frequently do a house cleaning, getting rid of all kinds of stuff that most people would probably keep forever, and other people may have been interested in possessing as collector's items. This includes other film-based items I have been questioned about including the sunglasses and the suit I wore in *Roller Blade Seven,* my rollerblades from the film, the frog masks from *Max Hell,* (that were also used in *Hell Comes to Frogtown*), the chupcabra costume (that cost like thirty-grand to have made), and so on. In fact, I can't even tell you when I tossed most of that stuff. For me, the clearing out of stuff is a very freeing, cathartic experience. ...Getting rid of the old energy and allowing the new to come in.

The sword I actually kept for quite awhile. In fact, it is the sword I used in the climactic scene in *Vampire Abstracta* AKA *Vampire Sunrise.* Just prior to filming that movie I found it hiding in storage and I decided to give it one more appearance on the silver screen.

The fact of the matter is, by then, (actually by way back in the way back when), the sword was pretty trashed and falling apart. Though it was an interesting piece in my cinematic history, I knew it was time to let it rest. So, after filming *Vampire Abstracta*, I took it apart, said a few mystical prayers over it, thanked it, and I said my goodbyes. Then, I sent it to sword heaven in the never-never-land of the Zen Films forever. So, to the potential buyer, *"Sorry, it is no more. Though believe me, if I still had it, I would have happily sold it to you for the amount you offered."*

In any case, life moves on. I try not to be bound by THINGS. If you are, then you are always worried about those items getting damaged or stolen. I try to live my life a bit freer than that.

Legend of the Roller Blade Seven

As I have stated in the past, it is almost scary, but I so often receive questions and comments about *Roller Blade Seven* and its offshoots that, not only does it dumbfound me, but I find that I must keep detailing the inside story of the film's creation, its attributes, and its incarnations. So, here we go again...

As I detail on the page of my website devoted to the *Roller Blade Seven* and more expansively in the chapter I wrote on the creation of the *Roller Blade Seven* in my book, *Zen Filmmaking*, *Legend of the Roller Blade Seven* was created by taking footage from the films, *Roller Blade Seven* and *Return of the Roller Blade Seven* and then, under the guidance of the executive producer, reediting the footage into another film, breaking all contracts that Donald G. Jackson and I had signed. In the reedit process, they also added some additional footage of Rhonda Sheer that Don and I didn't like or find appropriate for the films in order to give her a bigger part so it could be shown on her television show, *Up All Night,* on the USA network.

Just a note: Rhonda is a great person, and this discussion is no reflection upon her.

In any case, Don hated the new version of the film. Me... Well... It pissed me off a little bit that the executive producer had pull my producer, soundtrack, and screenwriter credit in that version of the film, (as much of the dialogue came from two books I had written), but overall, I didn't hate it the way Don did. Yeah, we were violated. Yeah, we were cheated. Yeah, it killed our vision.

Yeah, virtually all of the edits were mine; they were simply rearranged by somebody else who knew how to use editing equipment. But, this is Hollywood. And, getting cheated is a way of life. You are either cheating somebody or they are cheating you.

Hell, even though this version of the movie, a film entirely created by the blood, sweat, and tears of Don Jackson and myself, was shown on national/international TV several times, we never got paid a dime. Who did? The executive producer. Again, this is Hollywood.

On the day Don called me to drive him to the U.C.L.A. Medical Center where he spent the last days of his life, the first thing he said to me after I helped him into my car was, *"I'm really sorry about what happened to you on Roller Blade Seven."*

This was many years after the fact. Yet, my never getting paid while filming, and my never making any money from the film's distribution after the fact, truly bothered him.

By that point, I had moved on. But, I did appreciate him saying that.

The Roller Blade Seven and, as such, *Legend of the Roller Blade Seven,* have become Cult Classics. Cult Classics, for all the wrong reasons, I believe. They have been compared to *Plan 9 From Outer Space* and other such films. But, those who have critiqued RB7 in this manner have based their criticism upon not understanding what we were attempting to do. And, this is not an excuse. This is fact.

Knowing and having worked with one of the stars of, *Plan 9 From Outer Space,* Conrad

Brooks, I can tell you with some authority that Ed Wood was attempting to present his interpretation of Cinematic Art. He did this, as most independent filmmakers do; confined by the budget he had on hand. And, this is what Don Jackson and I did with RB7. We made the purest form of Cinematic Art that we could. We did this by intentionally stepping as far beyond the boundaries of budget, technology, and accepted filmmaking techniques as we could.

Whereas RB7 was made with Cinematic Art as the central focus, *Legend of the Roller Blade Seven* was not. It was reedited in an attempt to make the film more marketable.

Whenever something is made for marketability, art is lost. But, the truth be told, did the conversion of RB7 to *Legend of the Roller Blade Seven* work? Obviously not. It was the same movie, simply reedited with some added narration. Yet, the criticisms remained the same.

As one of the two filmmakers directly involved with the creation of *Roller Blade Seven*, I have always focused my attention upon the true versions of RB7 and *Return of the RB7*, not *Legend of the Roller Blade Seven*. That being stated, the good news is, the true *Roller Blade Seven* was the film released around the globe. But, here in the U.S., it was *Legend of the Roller Blade Seven* that found the wider release. Playing first on, USA Network's, *Up All Night*, and then on a few other networks, as well as it being widely released on videotape. (Anybody remember videotape?)

A lot of people who sees the RB7 related movies get what we were doing and really like them. These are the people who ask me, *"How did you get that camera angle or how did you make that shot?"* Then, there are those who don't.

The critics seem to be much more vocal than those who appreciate the film. But, I guess, that is always the case of life.

I think the biggest problem with RB7, (if there is one) is that it is one of those spaces in time where, if you weren't there, you may never get it. If, on the other hand, you were present during the filming and editing process, then you understand what was taking place. If you were not, and if you don't have an eye for Abstract Cinematic Art, then its essence will escape you. If you are one of those people then it becomes just another bad low budget film. But, for the person with the Artistic Cinematic Eye, RB7 has a lot to offer and a lot to be studied as can be seen from all the correspondence I receive regarding the film more than twenty years after its creation.

In closing, if you want to know what really went on, view the documentary I made last year, *Roller Blade Seven: The Unseen Scenes.* There you will not only see tons of behind-the-scenes footage, plus lots of the footage that didn't make it into the film(s), but I also tell some really interesting stories about the creation of what has now become a Cult Film Classic.

The Roller Blade Seven... I guess it has become a legend in its own weird way.

POST NOTE:
In 2015, with VHS long gone and the Executive Producer's company long ago in financial ruin, I decided it was time to put a new face upon *Legend of the Roller Blade Seven.* As such, I rereleased

Legend of the Roller Blade Seven with the original, edited by yours truly, footage of RB7. Sometimes it takes a long time to make things right but if you can wait it out, you can make it happen.

Max Hell Frog Warrior:
The Evolution

Max Hell Frog Warrior has an interesting set of circumstance that set its creations in motion. Certainly, its evolution goes back to *Hell Come to Frogtown.*

In brief, Frogtown is a geographic region of Los Angeles. It first became named this, when it was overrun with frog in the 1930s. A friend of Donald G. Jackson's, Sam Mann, lived in this area. As the story goes, one day they were driving around discussing movie ideas and Sam came up with the title. As he had already starred in Don's *Roller Blade* and *Roller Blade Warriors,* he was the obvious choice to perform the roll of Sam Hell, the lead character of the film.

Don planned to finance the film with his credit cards as he had done with *Roller Blade.* In the interim, he became involved with *New World Pictures,* and the offered to finance it for him. The only problem was, he had to add a completely different cast. His actor/friends were to be replaced by, "*Name Actors.*" Sam, the actual source of the concept was to be replaced by the then very famous wrestler, Rowdy Roddy Piper. Don asked Sam for his approval, which he gave.

Until his dying day, Donald G. Jackson regretted this decision. He felt bad for Sam being replaced. And, the movie was eventually taken away from his creative control.

Five years later, Don and formed an alliance with an executive producer who had a financier in place who was willing to bankroll their first film(s) as an executive producer. As she had a relationship with Don, they moved forward and created *Frogtown II*. Again, much of the creative control was taken away from him. He was left with a film that he never liked.

During this same period, just after the completion of *Frogtown II*, the executive producer wanted to finance another Jackson film. He offered up his *Roller Blade Series*. The 1991 outcome was the first and second Zen Films, *The Roller Blade Seven* and *Return of the Roller Blade Seven*, created by Donald G. Jackson and Scott Shaw

After the completion of those two films, Shaw took the foundations of *Zen Filmmaking* and went off on his own and created, *Samurai Vampire Bikers from Hell* and other films. Jackson also went on to create several script feature films of his own.

In 1995, Shaw was in Thailand. Jackson contacted him to reconnect and make another feature film. When Shaw returned, the two set about creating the next Jackson/Shaw Zen Film.

Initially, they team toyed with the idea of creating a humorous filmed based on Jackson and Mann's, *Hell Comes to Frogtown* theme, titled, Road Toad. This film was to star Scott Shaw and co-star Julie Strain. The team eventually discarded this idea and then set about on the idea of, *Hell Comes to Hog Town*. This film was to be based on the intent of Don Johnson's early starring role in the film, *Zachariah*, the First Electric Western, (which starred a young Don Johnson). This film would have Shaw ridding in, (with an electric guitar strapped over his shoulder), on the 1966 bright yellow, Harley

Davidson, Electra-Glide, he owned at the time. He would then battle the forces of evil that were controlled by an evil warlord known as, The Hog. Eventfully, this storyline was also put to rest.

What emerged from this period of creative interaction was Jackson's desire to do the story he had hoped to present with the original, *Hell Comes to Frogtown;* the story of a frog plague being unleashed by an evil overseer who would eventually be destroyed by the antihero. Enter, *Toad Warrior.*

Toad Warrior went up in the winter of 1996. In association with Jackson as the Producer/Director, Shaw was to perform the lead and Co-Produce/Co-Direct. The team of Jackson and Shaw brought on their friend and frequent collaborate, Joe Estevez, to play the Bad Guy. They also brought on Jill Kelly, who had initially appeared in *The Roller Blade Seven* and had since gone on to become a major force in the adult film industry. They also brought into the production Selina Jayne and Roger Ellis, both of which had appeared in the Roller Blade Seven and had starred in Shaw's *Samurai Vampire Bikers from Hell* and *Samurai Johnny Frankenstein.* The production went up in 1996.

Jackson and Shaw filmed, Toad Warrior in the high deserts of California and various locations throughout Hollywood, Los Angeles, and at their production offices in North Hollywood. Quickly, the production began to express and represent all the aspects of the bizarre *Zen Filmmaking* minds of the Jackson/Shaw team.

When production was complete, the team quickly moved onto other filmmaking projects. The next on the production schedule was *Shotgun Blvd.* AKA *Armageddon Blvd.* followed by *Ride with Devil.*

As the 1997 American Film Market was approaching, the production team of Jackson/Shaw knew they had to compete several projects. Shaw took on the editing of Armageddon Blvd and Ride with the Devil, while they turned *Toad Warrior* over a longtime friend of Jackson, and the editor of a number of his films AKA Christopher Blade.

The 1997 American Film Market premiers several Jackson/Shaw films. The one's named above and a long-form trailer of the film they were still working on, *Guns of El Chupacabra.*

Though the team was happy to have, *Toad Warrior* edited and available, it was never the film that they had hoped to make. Though the needed footage and scenes were all there, they were not constructed in the manner the production team had hoped. Though buyers from Malaysia and the Philippines purchased the rights to release the film and distribute it in their country, Jackson and Shaw, held back on U.S. sales as they wanted to reedit the movie.

The following few years proved to be very busy for the filmmaking team of Jackson/Shaw. Though they had hoped to get back to the film, *Toad Warrior* and re-edited it, this never came to pass. Shaw did, however, condense the original edited footage of the film into what the team called, a Zen Speed Film, and released with the title, *Max Hell in Frogtown.*

By the early part of the twenty-first century, Jackson had become very ill from his battle with leukemia and passed away in 2003. Soon after this, a distribution company somehow came by a beta master of the film, *Toad Warrior*, and released it in a compilation DVD. Many of the titles and screen credits were incorrect. Due to copyright infringements, his DVD was eventually removed from the market. But, this point in time, Shaw had already revamped the film and had released it as, *Max Hell Frog Warrior*. As the bootlegged version of the film had already been released, Shaw decided it was best to release the authorized version of *Toad Warrior* in order to help in counteracting any further distribution of this unauthorized version.

As of 2012 Shaw still plans to go back into the original footage of the film, reedit it, and that Jackson and he had hope for.

In recent years, there has been an ongoing interest in the film. Similar to the Jackson/Shaw creation of, *The Roller Blade Seven*, *Max Hell Frog Warrior* has continued to draw interest from critics and cult movie viewers. So much so, that the writers of the HBO television series, *Newsroom*, mentioned Max Hell in an episode of the show in August of 2012.

Shaw plans to take the franchise to the next level and create *The Further Adventures of Max Hell*.

Growing from the mind of Donald G. Jackson, the Frogtown series shows no signs of being forgotten in the near future.

SECTION V:
Inside Hollywood: Editorials

Hollywood's Just a State of Mind

I have often written about the subject of people who come to Hollywood to make it in the film, music, comedy business, or whatever. These pieces have been published in numerous magazines and books over the past twenty years.

I don't write these pieces so much as a warning – because we have all heard of the horror stories. Instead, I write these pieces to bring people's attention to the reality of what actually goes on here in Hollywood, (and I use Hollywood as a generic term).

The main thing I have continually stated is that pretty much everybody who comes to Hollywood expects to make it big overnight. A very few do. In fact, most do not. The ones that do make a name for themselves have luck, something unique to offer, or they figure out how to work their way into the system. The ones who don't, don't.

Though the reality is, if you ask anyone why they have come to Hollywood they will say, *"I have something unique to offer."* So much for people's beliefs in themselves. But, anyway…

Some of the people I have watched make a name for themselves have really surprised me. They came here and they actually accomplished something. Good for them! But, the ones who have made the films, got the roles, and so on, have one very important distinction—virtually none of them ever made any money, (or at least not much), from what they created. And, this is one of the sad truths of Hollywood—the Worker Bees, the one's who actually make things happen on an independent, creative level, rarely get paid.

That's not right but that's just the way it is... I even know a couple of *Academy Award* and *Grammy* winners who can only afford to live in dumpy little apartments.

On the other hand, you can come out here and if you continually hustle and work very-very hard to get your foot in the door you can work on a set as a grip, gofer, or even an extra. In these vocations you will get paid, at least a minimal amount of money. But, people don't come out here for that. They come out here to be a star. At every *Starbucks* in and around Hollywood you will see people sitting there writing a screenplay on their laptop. Think how many unproduced screenplays are out there. Yet, people continue to type away...

As I have detailed a thousand times, as a filmmaker I have spoken to so many people who bring up this person or that person who did make it big. *"I'm going to be like that."* Maybe... But, probably not. Of every person who has ever said that to me, I have never seen one of them do anything with their career. That is something to keep in mind because I have been doing this for a long time.

This being said, there is a reality; if you are a very passionate filmmaker, you can make a movie wherever you live and it may pave a road for you. But, the truth is, there are a million more opportunities here in Hollywood than exist anywhere else in the world.

The other side of this issue is, people who are somewhere else, may have all kinds of ideas of what goes on here but they actually have no factual basis for what they believe. They think this would happen or things should be this way or that. But, they are not HERE; they do not understand the reality of HERE. As such, they are just talking and saying nothing.

So, if you wish to know the reality of HERE, you need to be HERE. And, I don't mean come here and walk down Hollywood Blvd. or go to a club on the Sunset Strip. Come here and try to accomplish something creative. Stop talking about what you wish could, would, or should happen. If you want to know Hollywood, you need to live Hollywood.

In closing, if I can quote a line I fed one of my actors in one of my early Zen Films, *Samurai Vampire Bikers from Hell*, "Hollywood... Hollywood's just a state of mind."

Hollywood: The Impossible Game

People come to Hollywood everyday hoping to become stars. Once here, they pay hundreds of dollars to get headshots, pay thousands of dollars to take acting classes from teacher who, themselves, have never appeared in film, TV, or commercials to any substantial degree, if at all. Then, if the person is lucky enough to get an agent, they will buy clothing for auditions that they have no hope of getting, believe that they are actually appearing in something when they are only an extra in a film or on a television show, (FYI it is very easy to get extra work), buy video cameras to practice in front of, and this list goes on and on.

As someone who was born in Hollywood, I have a bit of unique perspective. In fact, I used to walk to *Hollywood High School* down the boulevard of the stars every day until I got a car and then I drove down Hollywood Blvd. to get to school. I lived between Hollywood and Sunset Blvd. So, I saw all of it, the whole Hollywood game from a very inside perspective. This is what caused me to never want to be involved in the film industry. But, I too fell prey to many of the drawbacks once I gave into the curse when I thirty-two years old. In other words, I know what it's like. The stories I could tell you...

All this is also why I go out of my way to help young actors and filmmakers wherever I can—because I know that most who come here will never achieve anything except maybe an overextended credit card bill.

Like I always tell young actors and actresses who delve into the indie film market, ninety-nine percent of the people who hope to make a film will never complete it because they do not have the focus, the finances, or the dedication to do it, so be careful. This same premise is why I developed *Zen Filmmaking.* To help those young filmmakers get past some of the hurdles and actually make their dreams become a reality.

But, let's face facts; Hollywood is an impossible game. Sure, some people do come from nowhere and actually make-it. Good for them! But, what is the truth behind their success? We will probably never know.

And, think about this, how many actors who had a TV series that you really liked or where in a movie that you remember, disappeared and were never heard from again. They had success for a second and then they were gone. Where did they go?

That is the truth about Hollywood; many people come here, most leave with only broken dreams. The others may have a moment of success and then they are gone. The few who make it, by talent, luck, karma, whatever, are the blessed ones. But, the main thing is, if you come here; never fall under the illusion that anyone or anything—that any about success will make you more than you already are.

Success is internal. Everything else can be taken away from you or it can simply fade away.

Hollywood, it is an impossible game. Fortunately, or perhaps more than likely, unfortunately; it is where I am from.

Like the line I fed one of my actors in the Zen Film, *Samurai Vampire Bikers from Hell*, *"Hollywood? Hollywood's just a state of mind."*

Film Reviews: Fact or Fiction

Ever since I first got into the filmmaking game I quickly began to realize that a lot of the magazines and even the authors of books put out fiction and claimed it to be fact. This has really intensified at the point when everybody got a voice on the internet. You don't have to have any credentials anymore, so all kinds of people began saying all kinds of things—many of which had absolutely no basis in fact.

When magazines and books began to discuss my films, back in the early 1990s, I quickly realized that many of them did not check their facts at all! They were stating a lot of things about my films, their development, who did what, and why, and all the etcetera... But, they were totally wrong!

I think most people do not realize this. They read what they read and instantly believe it. It's in a magazine, it's in a book, or even, it's on a website – it must be true; right? No, many times it is not.

And then, reviewers have gone on to misquote me and my associates; taking our words out of context and then writing a whole piece about what we or I said in order to get their own point of view across and somehow gain validity for it by jumbling the words of their source. That is just hatchet journalism. And, I can say that with some authority as I have had well over a thousand articles published and none of my editors would ever have let me do that.

I have long thought to write a piece titled, *"Reviewing the Reviewers."* I am sure I will get around to that at some point.

Perhaps the biggest fault of those who write on the subject of film is that they base what they write upon their own appraisal of a project. They are not so much presenting the reality of the film or of a filmmaker's process but, instead, they write what they think about the project and then disguise it as a literally discussion.

A few of the funny things that come to mind that authors and reviewers have gotten totally wrong about my films are: one author totally got the title of The Roller Blade Seven wrong in his book, *"Blade of the Roller Seven."* One magazine article said that the frog masks we used in *Max Hell Frog Warrior* were poor imitations of the ones uses in *Hell Comes to Frogtown.* In fact, they were the exact same masks! One author claimed that the Asia scenes in *Undercover X* were actually filmed in L.A.'s Chinatown. I guess he didn't take the time to read the writing on the signs or view the license plates on the cars. That was Tokyo and Seoul! One of the funniest, at least to me, was one author in his book detailed that one of the lead characters in *Killer: Dead or Alive* was my wife. I'm sure the actress that played that part was surprised to find out that we were married.

Those are just a few examples... It goes on all over the place.

And, on the internet, oh my god! The totally wrong things that they write and say...

Personally, I find all of this amusing. Some of my filmmaking friends are not so jovial as I am and get really upset.

But, this is the reality of life. People say or write what they write from their own perspective. And now, in the digital age, Andy Warhol's prediction has come to pass, *"Everybody gets fifteen minutes of fame."* Some people just choose to gain theirs by reviewing and discussing the works of others. And, in many cases, they base what they say upon fiction, not fact.

Reviewers:
Getting it Right. Getting it Wrong

When you create something it is always curiously interesting to find how other people view it. When you create something with art as a basis; be it a painting, a piece of literature, a photograph, or a movie, mostly people describe how they feel about it—if they like it or if they do not.

As we all come at art from our own preconceived notions and personal tastes, I always find it curious how other people come to define my work. Sometimes they get it right. They understand what I was doing. Other times they get it wrong.

At the source point of art, I guess that is the basis. The creator understands what they are doing and why they are doing it. And, in most cases, the creator likes what they have created. Someone who was not involved in the creation—someone who has no vested interest in the work, may not understand the creative source-process and they may not like it. That's just life. That's just art and the interpretation thereof.

As I have written in various places in the past, I have often thought about writing a piece called, *"Reviewing the Reviewers."* As many of my films have been reviewed in magazines, books, and on the Internet over the years, I find it very interesting when the reviewer gets things right and more particularly when a reviewer get things wrong but yet presents their words as facts.

Now, I'm not speaking about when people hate my films and totally rip them. That's fine with me. If you don't like it, you don't like it. Whatever... I'm speaking more of when someone who does not possess all of the facts presents the overall process incorrectly. But, none-the-less, writes as if they do.

Recently someone sent me a copy of a book where the author mentions a couple of my films and one film made, (at least in part), by my *Zen Filmmaking* friend, Donald G. Jackson (RIP). The book was pretty good. My stuff got discussed in the, Honorable (and Dishonorable) Mention Chapter. That was fun and amusing. But, the author got a few things wrong. Let me explain...

In one chapter, he discussed Don's film, *Pocket Ninjas*. I believe he got his source information from the Internet, because he states that Don and the executive producer were trying to make *the Roller Blade Seven* for kids. This is not true. This was not at all the basis for that film, though I have seen it detailed as such on the Internet. Don was simply obsessed with roller skates and later roller blades from the 1970s forward. He came up in the era of pretty girls on skates. So, he would integrate that into his films whenever possible. Plus, though he never personally trained, he loved the martial arts. As such, he would also feature the martial arts in his movies wherever possible. Thus, was the basis of *Pocket Ninjas*.

The author also attempts to detail the relationship between the executive producer and Don in the book. Again, I guess he got the information from the Internet because it mirrors what I have seen but it is essentially wrong. The executive producer did not come to Don; Don had our friend Mark Williams (RIP), write a script based on an idea he had. He then took the script to the executive producer.

I had previously worked with the executive producer, and he is a very nice guy. Don had also known him for years.

The executive producer was a formalized filmmaker; he had no intention of making a Zen Film. Pocket Ninjas was in no way a Zen Film. Bad, yes. But, not bad because it was a Zen Film.

In the book, the author details Don's removal from the film. But, he gets it wrong. The reason for the relationship collapse, and Don being pulled, was that the executive producer felt Don was letting production fall behind. Don, on the other hand, blamed the producer, who became the credited director. It was one of those common Hollywood dilemmas. Nothing-new here... But, we all still remained friends.

That's the story. I hope the world will finally get it right.

The author also makes an attempting at describing *Zen Filmmaking*. Certainly, I realize that is a bit of a complicated matter. ☺ And, the problem is, most people who talk about it, don't really get it. But, this author provides a fairly good overview. Good job!

He also discusses *The Roller Blade Seven and Max Hell Frog Warrior;* explaining that they are two of the best-known Zen Films. Maybe...

Roller Blade Seven is certainly, without a doubt, the most well know Zen Film, as it was released theatrically, on TV, and by other methods around the world. Actually, *Max Hell* is somewhat lowered down the list. Here in the U.S.

there has been a certain amount of talk about the film. They even mentioned it on the HBO TV show, *The Newsroom*. Thanks! But, the fact is, other Zen Films such as: *Samurai Vampire Bikers from Hell, Guns of El Chupacabra, Undercover X, Hitman City, Vampire Blvd., Vampire Noir,* and *Super Hero Central* have been much more widely distributed. But, that fact would be impossible to know unless you asked me.

In his description of *Zen Filmmaking* the author details that in *Zen Filmmaking* shots are often repeated. The fact is, to date, this is only true in the two films he mentions. It is not a common trait of *Zen Filmmaking.* The basis for this technique being used in the two discussed films is, *Roller Blade Seven* was the first Zen Film. We set up that film-style in that movie which we created in 1991 and 1992. Don and I did not make another film together until 1996 when we created *Toad Warrior,* which later became *Max Hell Frog Warrior.*

When we reconvened as filmmakers, we decided we wanted to capture some of the essence and energy of *Roller Blade Seven,* which is why I wore basically the same outfit, and we again employed that editing style. But, no other Zen Film that Don and I made as a team or that I have made employs that editing technique.

This is the thing about those who watch a Zen Film, particularly the two that were detailed in the book; *Zen Filmmaking* is constantly evolving. Each film brings with it its own sense of creativity and artistic expression. And the two discussed films are very different from every other Zen Film ever made. Ultimately, that is the essence of *Zen Filmmaking*, embracing the moment and allowing the creative environment of each film to guide you down the road to cinematic enlightenment.

But, as was embraced by P.T. Barnum and Andy Warhol, *"You may have gotten few things wrong but thanks for the publicity, Mr. Author."*

imdb.com: Fact or Fiction

The Internet Movie Database or imdb.com is the worldwide source for information about film and television production. But, just like *Wikipedia*, much of the information provided to imdb.com is done so by people who possess minimal or highly biased knowledge about a subject. In the case of imdb.com, the majority of people who submit or alter information were not actually a part of the production that they are submitting to. As such, they possess, at best, a limited knowledge and understanding about that production. From this, just like on *Wikipedia*, a lot of information on imdb.com is highly biased and, in some cases, just plain wrong!

Let me step back in time for a moment...

A programmer named Col Needham launched imdb.com in 1990. By the early 1990s it quickly becoming the industry standard for film and television information on the internet. Back then; as everything was in DOS, if you wanted to submit any new information or changes to imdb.com, it had to be done in a very precise manner that Needham's program would understand. This generally meant submitting the information several times before it was deemed ready to be uploaded. It was a real hassle!

Back then, anybody could submit anything. So, there was a lot of self-publicity going on and there were a lot of films posted that were never actually made. But, that's Hollywood.

As imdb.com's protocol loosened, this is where the real problems began.

I'm not going to bore you with the numerous stories I have about haters or people who didn't know anything about what I was doing but would do things like have my movies removed or they would combine two of my films under one title, they would also remove and/or alter credits, and all kinds of stupid stuff like that. And, this is not just about me, everybody I know who is in the game experienced the same set of occurrences. The problem was, as submitting was so difficult, getting stuff fixed or put back up, once it had been altered or removed, was a big-big hassle. In fact, in the later 90s there were actually companies set up that promised to fix your imdb.com info. ...For a price, of course.

As there are so many shenanigans that go on upon imdb.com, I sometimes get contacted by people asking me if something on the site is true or false—either about my films, my cast, my crew, or about me. The fact is, there have been so many mistakes up there over the years that I rarely even bother to check any more. But, whenever I do, there are a lot of inaccuracies.

The reason for this, I believe, is that, in some cases, people are trying to get their assumed knowledge about films out there. That's great! But, this being said, many times they are wrong. I know I have seen numerous inaccuracies put up in association with films I have created.

Then, as mentioned, there are always the haters out there. They submit things just to fuck with people. Uncool!

And, of course, this being Hollywood, there are always people who try to get their film or themselves mentioned in association with some big film or big star in order to get some free publicity. This forever makes me smile. ...My advice, regarding this practice; go do your own stuff and make yourself worthwhile instead of piggybacking on top of someone else!

There's also reviews and discussions about film projects and people on imdb.com. I always find reviews, especially negative reviews, funny—as reviews are just a way for the adolescent and adolescent minded people, with nothing better to do, to vent and get their frustrations out. But, here again, lies the problem with imdb.com; many of the things stated in these reviews are just plain wrong. For example, regarding my films, they have been wrong about my methodology, my equipment used, my locations, you name it... But, such is the truth of the internet.

Though my personal opinion is that imdb.com should only allow the Producer of a film to submit or alter information about a project, I am sure this is not going to happen anytime soon. And reviews... Well, reviews are just reviews...

All this being said, as someone who has made a lot of films, I can tell you to be skeptical about the information you find on imdb.com. A lot of times, it is incorrect. And, to this day, getting things fixed on imdb.com can be insanely difficult and time consuming. So, like all things on the internet, (and in life), see something for what it is and do not put your faith in a false god.

And, please people, unless you a fixing an obvious, *"Fuck you,"* stop altering other people's film listings. If they are up there the way they are, that is probably for a reason. Stop believing that you know more about a film than its producer or its publicist.

Everybody Wants To Do Something But Nobody Does Anything

I cannot tell you how many times I have heard a person telling me, I want to do this, or I want to do that. They talk and talk but they never get anything accomplished. In the film industry, I have been to so many meeting where someone wants someone to write a script or shoot a film. Again, talk and talk, meeting after meeting, but nothing gets done.

An ideal example of this took place way back when I was first getting my feet wet in the industry. A friend brought me into a deal he was setting up. The central figure of this deal was a lady who was the wife of some big player in the industry, and she was going to executive produce the film. After our initial meetings it was decided that my friend and I would write the screenplay and star in the film alongside some name actors. She brought in a, just graduated from U.S.C. guy, who was going to be the director and some other guy who was going to co-produce. We went through the story discussion meetings and then me, being who I am, I got the first draft screenplay written in about a day. Then we went through the rewrite meetings, the who was going to do what meetings, and all the etcetera meetings... Finally, we were all set to go. Of course, she didn't tell the would-be director that she wanted the film shot on some sixteen-millimeter film her friend had lying around. The new-be wouldn't hear of it. Thirty-five-millimeter only! You know, U.S.C. film school and all... So, after all the meetings, all the writing, after all the time and all the B.S., the deal fell apart. It all equaled nothing. And, this is just one example. There are a lot of others I have lived.

This is one of the primary reasons that I developed and have continued to refine *Zen Filmmaking*. To remove as many obstacles from the filmmaking process as possible. The funny thing, at least to me, is that so many people who have no true understanding of filmmaking or *Zen Filmmaking* have used my ideologies as a means of criticism. But, most of them have never even made a movie. Not a real film. Yet, they talk and talk and claim they will someday make one. Let's see it!

Like I have long said, *"Most people would rather critique than create."* It is a hell of a lot easier.

But, the desire to do, versus the actual doing goes so much farther than the film industry. So, many people want to write books, but they don't sit down and do it. So many people want to paint but they don't. People want to open restaurants, martial art studios, go back to school; all this and more. But they do nothing but talk.

The biggest thing between talking and doing is just that. Anybody can talk. Anybody can desire. But, the actual doing takes an intense focus of energy. And, that is very-very hard. It is not easy. Most people do not have what it takes to muster the energy to make something happen. So, all they are left with are their words. Which ultimately mean nothing.

This is life, you have to decide, are you going to take the first step and then continue through with the next step and the next step until you finally accomplish your desired outcome? It's

not easy. But, what do you want your life to be?
    Instead of, *"Critique rather than create."* I suggest, *"Create rather than critique."*

You Weren't There So You Don't Know

I often become very amused, (and even occasionally annoyed), when I read stories that people have written about what took place during the creation of some of my films. These people have these whole elaborate dialogues taking place. The only problem is, they are universally wrong.

Those actions were never taken. Those words were not spoken. Those ideas were not discussed. And, those ideologies were never attempted to be actualized.

People have even gone as far as to write entire articles amount my films, my self, and my filmmaking partners—all in an attempt to totally berate and slam me. *Dudes...* If you are going to do that, at least get your facts straight!

You know, there has been something truly lost with the creation of the Internet. Sure, a lot has been gained. Everybody who wants to have one, can have a voice. And, that is great. But, what has been lost is the quest for TRUTH. People say anything, and they do not even care if they are right, wrong, lying, or simply presenting what they think, and wish occurred. It all is sounded with the same voice and it is all consumed without the presence of mind to confirm whether or not what a person wrote possesses any validity.

People hide behind the mask of fan, film geek, reviewer, intellectual; whatever... But, by whatever name they assign themselves, what they propagate is falsehoods hidden behind the guise of someone who has actually taken the time to write something. And, once they write what they write, someone else reads it and believes it, thus the lie is perpetuated.

The number one thing I have to say in response is, I spend my time creating self-developed art. What do you spend your time doing?

People... You weren't there, so you don't know. Stop writing about a subject where you have no factual basis for your conclusions.

Too Famous
*...**For All the Wrong Reasons***

I had an audition early this week for a Midwestern commercial. They had only called in a few people for the audition. I believe there were four others and myself. So, this was a tight call. A lot of times production companies will see hundreds of actors for a role. For this one, that was not the case—they were seeking someone with a very specific look.

A kind of interesting thing happened to me at that audition. I went in and they slated me. That is where they take a digital photo of you, they do an upward pan of your body, you show your profiles, and you tell them your name. All common stuff...

In the room of this casting session was the cameraman, (doing the filming), and over on the couch were the director and a couple of other people. They were probably representatives from the company that this commercial was being created for.

In any case, as always occurs, the cameraman asked for my name. *"Scott Shaw,"* I reply. I noticed when I said my name a guy on the couch nudged the director and gave a little point. He whispered, *"That's Scott Shaw..."* They looked at each other and then at me. Once the cameraman was done with his duties I receive a question from the director,

"You're Scott Shaw?"
"Yes."

A strange look comes over his face, and a moment or two passes.

"I really liked your book, "Zen O'clock."
"Thanks."

At that moment, I knew I was not going to get the gig. I knew this even though I still went through the motions and read for the role...

Obviously, what had happened is that my agent had submitted me and the casting director had brought me in due to my appearance. But, the casting director probably didn't read my name.

Here's the thing... Everybody who is not a part of Hollywood believes that fame and accomplishment is the end-all. Let me tell you, it is not. In fact, many times it works against you.

For example, this role called for a New Age Guru type. All good, I look the part. But, the problem is, they could never cast me because then it would look like the company was endorsing my books and me. Thus, I lost the role.

This is the same thing for the type of films that an actor does. For example, when I first stared out in the industry, (at the ripe old age of thirty-two), I initially worked in A-market roles or on indie films that were geared towards the mainstream. When Don Jackson decided he wanted me to star in *Roller Blade Seven*, I knew my career would be changed forever. Though that style of film was and is much more in-tune with how I see the cinematic arts, it is the kind of film that sets a precedent for your career. In fact, my friend Joe Estevez once said to me about *Roller Blade Seven*, "I'm surprised either of our careers *survived after doing that film."*

That is true. That film and that style of filmmaking has defined me, in the film industry, since the day it was released. Though I have occasionally been brought in to do roles in mainstream films, TV, and commercials here in the States since RB7, those castings were more based upon the way I looked rather than the anti-fame I gained from that film and the other Zen Films I have created.

This is an important thing to understand about Hollywood. The casting directors are not seeking talent. They are either going to cast people that are sent to them by powerful agents, who set the standards and pretty much define the film game, or people who have a very specific look needed for a specific role.

Though this is the case with Hollywood, Asia is a bit of a different story. For the most part, the powers-that-be there do not view the kind of films I make as a detriment. They simply see them as Comic Book Action Adventures. A style of film that is very common throughout Asia. And, my films have done very well there.

This being stated, the other side of the coin is that due to the type of films I make, I continually receive offers to be in obscure indie films made by other filmmakers. I always turn those offers down, however. As I forever jokingly state, *"The only bad films I'm in are my own."*

Plus, I believe Joe Estevez is the king of that genre. I certainly do not want to infringe upon his territory. ☺

Ultimately, fame and notoriety are an evil master. I remember back when Dennis Rodman was just veering off from the top of his game. He had done a film with Mickey Rourke and Jean-Claude Van Damme. Though around this time he had been released from the Lakers, he was still everywhere—all over the media. Some reported asked him, *"Why don't you get more film and television work?"* He replied, *"Because I'm too famous."* He would later use this same statement to define why the courts severally punished him for his illegal deeds. Maybe that is true. I don't know. But, it is true that fame, no matter from which area it comes, defines your life and it keeps you from moving forward because you will forever be defined by that definition.

In terms of Rodman, I'm glad he has found success in Reality TV And hey, he's now a friend with the leader of North Korea. ☺

Anyway, it is important to think about what you are doing. Many people come to Hollywood and only focus upon the A-Industry. I wish them all the best, but that is a near impossible nut to crack. As for the world of indie, the opportunities are greater if you have a look or a skill or if you are a woman willing to take off her clothing. But, whatever you decided to do, remember; once it is out there in the public eye; it is out there forever. Any noteworthiness or fame you obtain will define you. And, that will dictate your next set of available opportunities.

Understanding the Influences

For each person there are a group of influences that comes to shape who and what they become as an adult. Cultural, societal, religious, and peer group factors all help to set the stage for who we emerge as when we come into adulthood. This is also the case for the artist.

In ages gone past, change happened at a very slow pace. Cultural and artistic ideologies would remain unchanged for decades, if not centuries. But, as the human race moved through the twentieth century and into the twenty-first century, these changes have become more and more accelerated. For the artist, and particularly the filmmaking artist, things have changed very-very quickly.

It was less than a decade ago when videotape, as a filmmaking medium, was highly looked down upon. I would teach university classes on the subject and literally have to debate with my students, detailing that it would be the wave of the future. Few believed me. I remember stating in an interview back in 1992 that it would take some large film, to be shot on video, for it to change the minds of the masses. Those films have since been made and that time has come and gone. In fact, filming on videotape has now become the norm, even for many of the high budget productions. And, this trend will continue, at least until the next: newer, better, format is developed.

Just as various factors influenced our path to whom we have become as adults, so too is the case for the factors defining the filmmaker that has emerged in those of us who have followed this particular path of artistic creation. The fact of the matter is, however, as times and technologies have changed so quickly, the influences that one filmmaker drew from and was inspired by are quickly lost to the minds of the younger, next generation.

To illustrate this, there are films that have existed since the creation of the process that have continued to remain relevant as an instructional tool to each person who enters the filmmaking path. For whatever reason, they have stood the test of time and have been touted by the soothsayers as a product that is valid and worthy of study.

But, more to the point; yes, there are universally appreciate, interesting pieces of cinematic history, but most of these films are not the ones that have truly influenced and defined the next generation of filmmaker. Most filmmakers are defined by the subtle elements of film and television that touched them in their youth. This simply fact explains why each new generation of filmmaker rarely understands the influences of those who have walked the filmmaking path before them – because the times have changed so quickly.

For example, if you look at many of the sci-fi movies of the 1940s, 1950s and the episodic sci-fi television shows of the 1960s, the special effects look so simplistic compared to what is taking place with today's technology. But, at the time those productions were created, that was cutting edge technology and people were mesmerized by what they were witnessing. Thus, there are many filmmakers who still draw their primary influence from films and television made during that period of time.

On a subtler level, even acting for the camera has dramatically changed. When you view the productions of the 1930s, 1940s, and early 1950s, the acting style was much more deliberate and noticeable.

As a filmmaker and/or director, when you work with an actor from that era, it is very quickly realized that those actors operate from a different perspective. This is not good, nor is it bad, it is simply who they are, defined by the influences and interactions of the era in which they came of age.

These two small examples lead me to the point of this discussion. People, and particularly filmmakers, are defined by the visual images that they found appealing when they were in their youth. From this, they gained their inspiration and the insight to make movies in and of a particular manner.

In short, as filmmakers, we each possess our own set of influences. This is particularly the case in the independent film market, where the controlling hands of the production company or the producer are not so prevalent. Also in this independent arena, films are allowed to be made by and for people who seek out a specific subject manner, presented in a definitive manner. Due to this fact, those who have found their influences from a different, more modern period of time or from some different genres may be the first to find fault with a particular film or with a filmmaker's philosophy who bases their artistic expression upon a previous period of time. But, that is solely based in the fact that they do not understand a particular filmmaker's influences.

For better or for worse, filmmaking is an art form. For each piece of art, there will be admirers and there will be critics – that is simply the name of the game. But, if you desire to truly understand why a filmmaker makes movies in a specific manner, the only way to do that is to look into and come to understand that filmmaker's set of influences.

This fact also goes far beyond the arena of filmmaking. Life is defined by influences. Some are good. Some are bad. But, it is each of us we must decide which ones come to shape us and define our overall character both artistic and otherwise. Moreover, as each person is shaped by their own set of influences, if you wish to truly know a person; desire to truly understand them, you must first define, study, and then understand their unique set of influences.

Terminator 2

I am sometimes asked questions about my involvement with the movie, *Terminator 2*. To answer, it was kind of an interesting process. My involvement was somewhat interesting that is... Not so much my role in the film...

To the story...
I received an audition to be in the film. Auditions are a very common process in Hollywood. This audition came when I was very new to my acting career.

In my first year of acting, I found my niche in the action-adventure market and was trying to break into the mainstream. On my second or third audition, I got a role in the Bruce Willis, Tom Hanks movie, *Bonfire of the Vanities.* That role got me my SAG card, which is an absolute necessity if you want to work in Hollywood. I had a few projects that I was cast in after that and I continued to audition.

When I got the audition for *Terminator 2*, my agent didn't even tell me what it was for. I don't think she knew.

This is a very common practice in Hollywood, as the casting directors don't release the actual title of the project, especially when it is a high-profile project such as was the case of T2.

I went to the audition with my girlfriend. It was held in a building on Sunset Blvd. in Hollywood.

Most auditions happen pretty quickly, so I left her waiting in the car—thinking she would be waiting for a maximum of fifteen or twenty minutes. This was not a quick audition, however. I was in there, with other potential case members, for well over an hour and a half. In fact, I went to check on her a few times to make sure she was okay as I was awaiting my turn in the casting office. She was...

Finally, I got to go in for the auction. It was for a cyber-tech guy. The casting director liked my reading, liked my long blonde hair, and loved my glasses. I was out and onto the day with my girlfriend.

A week or so later, I was confirmed for the gig. It was only then that I found out it was for T2. *"Pretty cool,"* I thought.

The actual gig was not for a month or so in the future, however. In the interim, I did a TV show and continued to audition for other projects.

Somewhere in between the audition and my actual shoot date, my agent called me and told me that the T2 production team was looking for a few people with cool cars. She knew I had a 1964 Porsche 356 SC. She wanted to know if I was interested in driving my car in the film for, I believe, (if I remember correctly), $250.00. I didn't have any plans for the evening that my car was needed, so, *"Sure. Why not?"* I could make some money...

The call time was at 6:00 PM at an old bar in North Hollywood. For those of you who have seen the film, it is the bar Arnold goes into when his character first arrives.

I arrived that evening and was directed to hang out in the bar with some of the biker types until they were ready to shoot the scene with my car.

A funny incident occurred at one point that evening. Arnold walked into the bar. He looked around and said, *"Hi."* Due to the fact that all the bikers were too hardcore to acknowledge him, no one responded. He smiled and left. People...

Anyway, a bit later, maybe around 9:00 PM, the 2nd A.D. came and got me. He handed me a walkie-talkie, told me to go get my car, and pull it onto a nearby street in front of the camera truck. I start walking.

I get into my car and tried to start it...

For any of you who know anything about vintage cars, you know they are very temperamental. My 356 didn't want to start.

I was sitting there, completely freaking out, getting calls from the 2nd A.D. over the walkie-talkie, *"Where are you?"* This went on for what seemed like an eternity. Finally, I got my car to start, and I made it to the location.

There was Jim Cameron sitting on the camera truck. He positioned my car in association with a few other unique looking cars that were chosen for the scene. We started driving. Passing us, several times, was Arnold's stunt double, riding the Harley Davison motorcycle that was used in the film.

The process of starting, repositioning, and driving went on for a couple of hours. Jim Cameron got what he needed. I turned in the walkie-talkie and went home about 2:00 AM.

That car scene never made it into the final cut, however. But, this is not unusual in high-budget Hollywood productions. A lot of scenes are shot, but not all of them are used.

A couple of weeks later, my agent called me with my call time for the actual part I audition for. It was a night shoot, again, and the call time was in the evening.

The shoot was to take place at a set they had constructed inside a warehouse in the Valencia area of Los Angeles Country. It was near what is now called, *Six Flags Magic Mountain* for those of you unfamiliar with the area.

I arrived and checked in. Wardrobe did what they did to me. They had me wear my glasses. The ones the casting director had liked so much. Makeup did their job. They wired me for sound, and I waited.

My call to the set actually happened pretty quickly. Which is, in many cases, very unusual in big Hollywood productions. Sometimes, on high-budget sets, you wait for hours upon hours.

Anyway, they called me to the set and there was Jim Cameron. He is a very hands-on director.

At one point, he and I were in very close proximity to one another. There was my chance…

"You're a friend of Don Jackson, aren't you?"
"Yes I am." He firmly said.

I stated this because I knew that he and my friend, Donald G. Jackson had met while they were both working for Roger Corman. After that, Don had shot a bit of Terminator for him and he had shot a music video, that was directed by Cameron, for a band that actor, Bill Paxton, was in, Martini Ranch.

I continued,

"Yeah, I just did the lead in his next Roller Blade movie..."
"Is he still milking that?" Smiling concluded Cameron.

With handshakes out of the way, that was that...

He positioned me in a few different places for the scene I was to be in. He shot me walking and standing. He then told me what he wanted me to say, which was actually something different than was in my script. And, the scene was shot.

The overall process of the setup and shooting the scene took maybe two hours. Cameron had a stedicam operator, that shot the scene, and he was very happy that the scene went well and he could move on.

In the final cut of T2, you don't hear my dialogue but if you don't blink, you can see me for half a second. That's Hollywood for you... Sometimes movies need fillers. That's why they hire actors to do small parts. Just in case... But, as good as T2 is, it didn't need any filler. Though that was a bit of a disappointment to me; obviously... But, I did get to meet Cameron, one-on-one.

I was released soon after the scene was complete. It had begun to rain very hard in L.A. I walked out to my 356 and got in. Recently, I had pulled the rubber that lined my car's sunroof and had yet to replace it. My mistake. I drove home, and it was like taking a shower all the way down the 405 freeway headed towards the South Bay. I, and the inside of my car, got drenched.

So, for those of you who have asked, that's' the story…

The Only Bad Movies I'm In Are My Own

As I have become fairly well-known in the independent film game, both as an actor and a director, I frequently receive offers to appear in other people's films. Though I certainly appreciate all of the offers, I inevitably turn them down. As I always joking tell people, *"The only bad movies I'm in are my own."*

The reality is, people act in low budget, independent films based on two reasons. One, they hope to make money. Two, they need to be in a film to get tape on themselves to show their acting chops to agents and other filmmakers in order to move up the ladder. In my case, neither one applies.

The fact is, I am a member of SAG, the *Screen Actors Guild.* As such, I cannot be in a non-union film.

As virtually all films on the low budget, indie side of the picture are non-union, I can't be in one if I wish to maintain my relationship with and membership in SAG. I know many actors who have danced on the wrong side of this line, hoping to make some money, and they have all lost – they were kicked out of SAG.

As being a member of SAG is the only way to be in studio films, television shows, and commercials; membership is a must. They own the industry, and you just do not mess with this powerhouse.

As an actor, periodically I have been luckily enough to appear in studio films, TV shows, and commercials. In terms of acting, that is my bread and butter. So, I want to say, *"Thanks,"* to all the people who ask me to be in their non-union indie films. But, *"The only bad movies I'm in are my own."* ☺

Want To Be In A Movie?

As an established filmmaker I am periodically contacted by actors telling me that they are available and that they would like to be in one of my films. Now, in essence, this is all well-and-good, because, as a filmmaker, unless you want to use puppets to tell your story, you really have very few other options than using actors.

As I have long talked and written about, casting is one of the most complicated elements of filmmaking, particularly here in Hollywood, California. This is because of the fact that people from all over the world come here expecting to be stars. They all possess the same story and the same mindset that they deserve to, *"Make it."*

In fact, I wish them all the best. But, the reality is, very few will ever rise to the level of success that they feel they deserve.

Now, I won't go into it here, because I have documented the trials-and-tribulations of casting and dealing with actors in several other discourses, but what I will say is that casting actors is one of the most troublesome and time-consuming elements of filmmaking. This is mainly due to the reality of dealing with misplaced egos and the unfulfilled desires of the majority of people who call themselves actors. In other words, actors are a problem...

This being stated, one would think that a filmmaker being contacted by an actor, to be in a film, alleviates some of the problems of the casting process. And yes, to a degree, it does. For if an actor contacts me, I can expect that they understand the style of films I make and what can be expected on my sets.

There is a problem, however... Actors, whether they are cast through the traditional casting process or those who have contacting me, do not want to do anything. They want to show up, be treated like a star, and then be allowed to get in front of the camera and do their thing.

In reality, I suppose this is fine, because that is what an actor does—act. But, what most actors do not consciously understand is that there is a lot of preparation and planning that goes into the filmmaking process long before the cameras can roll. This is true even in *Zen Filmmaking*. When actors do not understand this, and are simply focused on themselves, they do not comprehend that there is a lot of work that must take place to actual deliver them to the audience as a believable character.

Some will say, *"That is the job of the filmmaker. Bringing together all of the elements of a film, putting the jigsaw puzzle pieces together, and then delivering a finished product."* This is true. But, let's look at this process from a more evolved perspective.

Think about it, what if the job of creating a film was not solely in the hands of the filmmaker? What if the actor, instead of only expecting to show up and act, decided to become part of the process? Would a film then not become more of a universally collaborative effort? And, from this, would the essence of each character, having brought something more than simply their body to the project, then have more consciously contributed to the overall whole of the completed film?

I am not saying that the actors should be allowed to direct a film that they are acting it. Nor, should they be allowed to alter the story. For then, everything gets convoluted.

I have seen so many films fall apart when this style of filmmaking is allowed to take place. What I am saying, however, is that actors, especially in the independent film arena, should stop thinking of themselves as a whole and complete commodity onto themselves. Instead, they should think about what they can bring to a project besides their acting.

If I can sidetrack here for a moment... One of the most common questions I receive as a filmmaker from an actor is, *"How much are you going to pay me?"* I commonly jokingly reply, *"How much are you going to pay me to put you in this film?"*

The reality is... And, this is something that most actors do not understand, is that their name means nothing to the sale of a film. Very few people, if anyone, is going to purchase or rent a film because an unknown actor is in it. Why people will purchase or rent a film, however, is the overall concept, title, or idea. For this reason, I virtually never pay actors. I believe that they are receiving payment enough by being given a change to be in a film.

This being stated, actors really need to start thinking about what they can bring to the table if they want to be in a film. For example, one actor I have frequently cast in my films has this great apartment in Hollywood, which we have used for a filming location several times. Other actors I have worked with have found various locations to film at. An actor/cinematographer I worked with had access to a warehouse. One actress I worked with on a few films was also a professional makeup artist. And, so on...

What I am saying is, actors need to quit thinking that being an actor is enough. What they need to do, in addition to acting, is bring a valuable commodity to the table, other than their acting chops. Now, this can be anything: locations are always a great contribution to the independent film, camera or lighting ability, organizational, or casting skills; all help. It can really be anything that will help the overall production and completion of a film. But, *"No,"* not a script! There are millions of those out there.

From my own personal perspective, from the moment I entered the film industry as an actor, I was always watching, learning, and trying to help out on the set. Sure, I would do my lines. But, if anything else needed doing; whether is was setup, teardown, holding a boom, running cable, laying dolly track, setting up lighting; I was there, always willing to help. And, I did this on both low and very high budget sets. From this, not only did I learn valuable skills but I also contributed to the overall production of the film.

In closing, what an actor must bring to the table in this modern, digital age is something/anything that will contribute to the overall production and completion of a film. From this, the actor becomes more than simply a guided talking-head, spitting out words. They become a true part of the filmmaking process.

Is That Who You Are?

A few years ago, I was sitting around having lunch with a friend of mine and he asked, *"Is that who you are? ...A Cult Filmmaker."*

For the record, I never considered myself, *"A Cult Filmmaker."* A *Zen Filmmaker,* yes. But, a *Cult Filmmaker,* no.

What I do is to make something out of nothing. I use available sets, urban and rural locations that I find visually interesting, create and guide the actor's dialogue on the spot, and make a film out of what occurs from this process.

Yes, my mind is a bit abstract, so I commonly, (but not always), explore abstract realms of reality in my films, but that does not make them cult. They simply are what they are.

As I am frequently questioned about this fact... The difference between the Zen Film that I have made and the ones that I made in association with Donald G. Jackson is that I am acutely organized and time orientated. I bring people on the set so they can work, get their part done, and then go home. Like I always say, *"Give me a few hours of your life and I will make you a star."* Don, on the other hand, was complete chaos. His idea was that we would congregate as many people as we could get, drive to far off locations in multiple cars, and then (maybe) the people who we cast would get a part in the film. But, many times they did not. Few ever got the part they thought that they would get. He did this, while spending all kinds of money, buying people all kinds of food and stuff like that.

A side note: (and I have mentioned this in other writings), Don was the biggest waster of money I have ever met. If he did not spend money on everybody and everything, he would have been quite rich. But, because he always paid for breakfast, lunch, and dinner for everybody, paid for the concerts, the clubs, the movies, the strip clubs, and everything else, paid for his various girlfriend's rent, and paid for more boob jobs than I can even count, he was most often broke. He did this, and no one ever appreciated what he was doing for them.

I learned from him though. I learned what not to do. It's just not fair to make people believe that they are going to get a part in a film, travel to a location, and then nothing—zero. And, it certainly is a waste of energy to spend all your money on people who do not appreciate it.

This is also why more films that involved Don Jackson came out after his death than while he was alive. We would film stuff, he would lose interest, then he would hide the footage away somewhere in his house. Nearing his death, he gave all the footage to me. Thus, all the movies we did could finally be constructed and completed. In fact, more than a decade after his life, I still have a few more to put together.

To me, this is the filmmaker I am. I get it done.

Anyway, that's just to answer or re-answer many of the questions I receive about what went on between Don Jackson and myself and how we were the same and/or different...

To the point... Like my friend, I understand that many people consider me a *Cult Filmmaker*.

But, here lies one of the key factors of life: people see you, the way they see you. They define you, the way they define you. That does not make their definition correct, however, that simply makes it their definition.

Who you are, is who you are, defined by what you do. If what you do causes people to have an incorrect opinion of you, you have two options. One, you can fight to make them understand. But, the reality of life is most people never step out of their own head long enough to truly understand anyone or anything. They see something, conceive their definition, and that is that. Your second option is the one I choose to employee – just be who you are. By encountering life in this manner, the people who are open and understanding enough will come to you and let you be who you actually are without attempting to define you by some incorrect definition.

Don't get caught up in seeking definitions, it makes life far too inaccurate.

When You Believe

I often speak about the downside of the film industry in an attempt to, if not protect people from the downfalls, then at least to warn them about what can happen. From my time at *Hollywood High School* onward, I have seen how the film industry has deceived many a person and has handed them belief but not the reality.

Personally, after receiving offers for many years to enter the film industry, I finally gave in at the ripe old age of thirty-two. I dove in headfirst. Looking back, I really should have become involved much earlier, as youth has a lot of benefits that are not possessed by the aged. But, when I was younger, I was doing other things...

Everybody wants to be a movie star, don't they? This is my belief. Most never possess the drive to go after this dream, however. But, some do. And, here is where the problems begin.

The thing about the film industry is that it is like this weird drug. There are all these promises—promise that never come to volition. But, once you step into the ring, they are always there, tempting you.

Producers and directors promise you roles in their films. Films that are never made. Auditions make you believe that you are getting somewhere. But, auditions are not being cast in a role. Being an extra (which anyone can do) on a big set makes you believe that you have what it takes as you are rubbing elbows with stars. You are in the same scenes with them, standing only a few feet away and all... But, the fact is, you are not one of them. You were not cast for your role they only put you on the set because you look the way needed to sell the live action and time period of the film. Ultimately, extra work only leads to more extra work. It is the biggest lie of all that it leads to anything more. This is why I don't use extras in my films.

Then, some people get roles in indie films. Most indie films do not pay but they are something. But, what is that something? Sometimes they are pure exploitation. Something you end up being quite embarrassed for even being a part of it. I have known beautiful young girls, (one in particular), that actually had sex on camera for a zero indie film. What did that equal? I also knew one girl in the U.S.C. School of Law who had her eyes on the prize of becoming a big lawyer but who was bitten by the acting bug and was persuaded to get naked on camera and simulate sex for a zero indie film. I am sure that has haunted her ever since.

The thing is that the film industry promises the ultimate illusion: fame, fortune, and stardom. All part and parcel of the ultimate American dream. But, for the very-very-very few that obtain it, most only look back with regrets.

In this day and age, making a film has become easier and easier. With this has also risen the number of films made by incompetent filmmakers. Incompetent filmmakers following the same dream to stardom and promising the same lies that have been handed down for a hundred years to the budding stars and starlets.

What does it all equal? Following a pathway of desire, dreams, and lies. None of them are healthy.

Hollywood is a no-win game with the ultimate promise of achievement. Be careful where you step.

Nobody Remembers Their Name

I often jokingly tell stories about some of the calamities I have encountered while casting a movie. Nobody ever believes me until they try to do it themselves. There have been so many times I have discussed this subject with students in my classes or at a seminar and there is always someone who is dismissive if not downright argumentative about the realities of casting an indie movie. Then, they try to bring-up a film and I always hear back from them telling me, *"You were right!"*

Hollywood is a strange beast. And, I use the term, *"Hollywood,"* to describe the film business in general. But here, in actual Hollywood, people come to be stars. They come to be stars on the big screen. And, they expect to have it happen overnight with no effort. They feel they have a look or talent and that should be enough. From my experience, I can tell, you it is not.

In any case, I have discussed some of the situations that have occurred while attempting to cast in a film in many other places. There is extensive discussions of the subject in my books: *Zen Filmmaking* and *Independent Filmmaking: Secrets of the Craft*. But, one of the ideal examples that comes to mind is when Don Jackson and I were originally going to film *Lingerie Kickboxer*. We planned to shoot it on 35mm and do it in a *twenty-four-hour* period just to show the world that it could be done. We had shows like *Entertainment Tonight* and reporters from industry magazines like *The Hollywood Reporter* scheduled to meet us throughout the shooting day at various locations. At 4:00 AM, the night before the shoot, I receive a phone call from the actress who was to play the lead role in the film, she told me she couldn't do it because she had to go to a family reunion with her boyfriend. Thus, the production came to screeching halt.

There have been numerous other times where I offered actors and actresses the lead or a supporting role in a film and they either didn't show up for the production or called me the night before saying they decided not to do it or their agent told them not to do it.

I won't even go into the bullshit-ness of agent here...

So, there went their roll. One of the more amusing phone calls I received was from one actress who called me up and rudely stated, *"I'm not going to be in a film just so you can have somebody make-out with me!"* What? She sure had a high opinion of herself. In any case, I had offered her the female lead in a film where all she had to do was kiss a guy to establish they were in a relationship. Not too much to ask for a starring role. And, this chick was a stripper by trade and had never been an actual film—even though her resume said she had.

Remember the number one rule of filmmaking, *"Everybody lies."* Anyway...

Aside from not showing up or not showing up on the next day of a shoot to complete their role, some people have left my set before they were even filmed due to the fact that they arrived and discovered that we were not a major Hollywood production. Though I certainly never claim to be.

Just a side note here: This is one of the problems that occurs from people being an extra in a movie or on a TV show. In those situations, the productions are BIG. Thus, the novice actor or actress comes to believe that all productions should be that big. From this, what happens is that their minds have been misled into believing that the BIGS are the only real productions. They are not.

All this being said, let me get to the point, because I could go on for hours upon hours about this subject... I have worked with a lot of very talented actors and actress since I enter the film industry many years ago. The majority of them are nice, professional, and came to do their job and did it with excellence. At the end of the day, they were in a movie. In fact, some have used this on-camera experience to springboard their careers. Others did not move up the ladder, but at least they have one film that they were in to show their family and friends.

I had a realization while I was driving this afternoon... It was, all of those people who turned down the opportunity to be in one of my films, (for whatever reason), I do even remember their name. And, nobody else does either.

You really need to accept opportunities when opportunities are offered to you in your life.

End of an Era

Sadly, the *Jaw of Cinema*, Robert Z'Dar passed away at the age of sixty-four.

I first met Z-Man, (as we came to call him), on the set of *Samurai Cop*. It was a strange meeting in that I knew him from A-films like *Tango and Cash* but was surprised to find him on this No-Budget set.

Samurai Cop was a film created by Amir Shervan. Shervan operated out of a junky, cluttered house on Beverly Blvd. in East Hollywood. He had called me in on the film, when I was first getting into the industry, because he didn't like the swordplay in his film and wanted me to make the samurai work look more realistic. He also offered me a roll in the film, as well. The cast was all very nice.

The cinematographer on the film was a man named, Peter Palian. Previously, Palian had been the personal cameraman for the *Shah of Iran*. But, as history tells us, the Shah was deposed. Peter was one of those interesting people in that he always wore a leather sport coat, a dress shirt with an ascot tie perfectly tucked into his shirt. He had a perfectly trimmed goatee and smoked a pipe. I would periodically bump into him around Hollywood. Nice guy.

On the first day I was on the set, instead of filming we went and had lunch at a burger joint. There is where Z-Man and I sat down and talked. Immediately, I understood he was a great guy!

The problem was, at least in terms of the film, we ate instead of filmed. It was getting late. By the time we got up to steal the hilltop location in Silver Lake, we were losing the light. As the movie was shot on 16mm film, this was problematic. Though I tried to guide Z'Dar in proper samurai sword usage, there wasn't time. Post that, I realized the film was just too clusterfuck for me to be a part of and I didn't return.

Soon after that, Z-Man and I worked together on the film, *Divine Enforcer*. We were the bad guys. We had a big fight scene with a bunch of opponents. It was fun.

After that Z-Man and I would sometimes hang out at places like *The Rainbow* on the Strip in the late hours of the evening, throwing back a few. He would always ask, *"You got any nose candy, Scotty."* The man did like his intoxicants.

Our paths, both as friends and as actors, continued to cross, whether it was on auditions on in films. He, of course, was the lead in *Frogtown II*. There were a lot of problems with that film. Not the least of which was the director, my *Zen Filmmaking* buddy, Donald G. Jackson. Sometimes he would get in a mood and treat the actors and crew very badly. This, when the fault was actually always with him. At one point Z-Man took his *Texas Rocket Ranger* helmet and threw it at Don.

Things also went sideways on my film, *The Rock n' Roll Cops,* where Don was the executive producer and the cinematographer. This event is discussed in an article written about the film that made it into my book, *Zen Filmmaking*. To tell the story, Don was in a mood. He apparently knew he was going to be an asshole and hired a professional bodyguard to go out with us. There we were on the roof of a parking structure in

Burbank, stealing the location. We had a lot of people with us, most of us with loaded guns. So, this was no joke and the vibes, due to Don's behavior, were very tense. He was yelling and screaming at the second cameraman, just treating him like shit. I asked the guy why he didn't leave. But, he wanted to be the, "Better man," as he put it. At one point Don starts screaming at Z-Man. *"I wish we could get a decent fucking actor on this set."* Z'Dar, always the gentleman, simply replies, *"I take exception with that, Donny."*

And, this is the thing, Z-Man was a great actor. I think some people never understood that all they defined him by was his face. But, he was a really good actor!

He was also the consummate professional. He could have kicked Don's ass, and I would not have stepped in. I doubt that Don's paid-for bodyguard would have helped either as he got freaked out by all that was going on and eventually bailed. But, Z-man worked with us until the early morning hours of dawn, when he finally got paid his $300.00 and went home.

You can see Don's obsessional camera work and Z-Man doing and redoing this one scene over and over again in the Zen Documentary, *Cinematografia Obsesion,* if you want to. Even after all this he remained friends with Don. I remember Z-man calling Don when he was in the last days of his life at U.C.L.A. Medical Center. Don apologized to him. Z-man told him not to worry about it.

Z-Man certainly etched his name into the world of Cult Cinema. I believe had he walked a slightly different path he could have maintained a career in the high budget market. But, he went astray of SAG. I don't know if he ever resolved that problem. The thing is, SAG, now SAG/Aftra, controls the mainstream industry. If you are not a part of it, you cannot work. As they are a union, they do not let their actors work in nonunion films. Yes, one can follow the path of Financial Core status, but that is only limited SAG membership and there are many detriments to that status. Z'Dar got caught working nonunion. SAG, if they find this out, expect you to pay all the money you earned on any film to them, plus a fine. The last I heard Z-man never paid that. But, he did have a wide spanning career.

Z-Man eventually moved back to his home in the Chicago area. He had inherited his mother's house. While in L.A., he, as many actors do, spent much of his time near penniless and couch surfing. Surprisingly, it was once he returned to the Midwest that he began to get tons and tons of work. I remember Joe Estevez telling me one time, *"He owns that town."*

I believe with the passing of Z'Dar it again signals the ending of an era. I wrote about this maybe a year or so ago when I discussed the fact that no new Scream Queen were moving to center stage to take over for the aging girls of the previous era. This too is the case with Z'Dar. It is a signal. And, I guess that's life, times and trends move on.

I look to the filmmaking that is going on, and yes there are tons of movies being made. But, few are following the path of true Cult Cinema. Some are imitation of, some are just bad movies, but few illustrate the market that Z-Man was one of the Kings of.

There are so many stories I could tell about Z-Man. But, I will leave it at this. You will be missed, Bobby. You were one of the greatest actors I have ever met and had the pleasure of working with.

Saying Everything That I Said

It is always amusing for me to listen to a person speaking, read the writings of a person, or the words that are spoken when an individual is being interviewed and they say exactly what I have already said but they claim it as their own ideology. It is strange... It is flattering, (I guess) ... But, it is also a bit disconcerting...

In fact, there have been a few people who while attempting to rip on me have actually stolen a passage I have written; word for word and have used it as if they invented it. I mean, if you are going to be critical at least think up your own things to say. ☺

But, let's get more to the point... If you are writing something that means you have something that you feel needs to be said. If you are being asked questions in an interview that means you have done something/accomplished something that others find worthwhile. All good...

The fact is, if you have done something worth doing you must first have a philosophy to guide you towards doing it. Most people have none. Thus, when they try to do something, they fail at it miserably. No philosophy equals no true expression of that philosophy. Thus, nothing can be created.

Okay... But, where did that philosophy come from?

We each are influenced by our time in history, other people, and the world around us. For those of us who have a creative mission in life, we do things that create an end result—an object, a thought, or a thing. Then, when we are asked how or why it is we, the creative proponent of that equation, created what we did, we must come up with an explainable logic that guided us to create our creation and how others may follow in our path if they hope to do something similar.

Certainly, I have written a lot about a lot of stuff. I have spelled out my, *"Why and How,"* for all that I do. I do that to help others overcome obstacles if they hope to follow a similar path. But, for those who take the understandings and philosophies that I bottled and then call it their own – I don't know? It is perplexing...

I think back to when my *Zen Filmmaking* buddy Donald G. Jackson was still alive and when we were interviewed, either as a team or as a separate entity, our answers were often times very similar. That was because we had created a movement together, *Zen Filmmaking.* We didn't base it on anything that had been done before. We based it on our own understanding of the NOW and the creativity of immediate inspiration; leading to cinematic enlightenment. Without our interaction *Zen Filmmaking* would never have happened. Yes, I was more literate on the subject and more focused on formalizing and presenting *Zen Filmmaking* definition to the world, but without our teaming up, it may never have been an actualized entity. So, when we said the same thing, it was expected. But, when others say what I have said, sometimes exactly—write what I have written, and don't throw me a bone, it is very surprising...

Like I have always said about *Zen Filmmaking, "Make it your own."* You don't have to do what I do, just do it. Remove as many obstacles as you can and do what works for you. But, I think I should also probably paraphrase here, if you are going to quote me, use my words and my philosophies, say what I have already said, at least throw me a bone and state where your words and/or your ideology came from.

The Scott Shaw Guide to Must See Cinema

There are a lot of great movies out there. This list is not made up of great movies, however. This list is made up of films that have helped to define a filmmaking genre, delineated an era, moved the understanding of filmmaking forward, or set the standard for how the next generation of film is created.

Though there are a lot of great movies, in a few cases, the ones listed below are not that great. What they are, however, is a film that has stood the test of time and can be seen as truly having influenced the evolution of filmmaking and the film-story process.

Certainly, it may be argued that truly revolutionary filmmaking has only taken place within the more esoteric realms of the industry. Though, in truth, the Art House films have been the one's to truly push the envelope of filmmaking forward. The fact of the matter is, the majority of these films are so obscure that they were never seen by the general film-going public. As such, though much of the true art of cinema was first presented in this genre, as these films were not widely seen or embraced, they did not and could not change the course of filmmaking history. Instead, it was the larger budget films, that drew from the influences of these films, that came to set the stage for the evolution of filmmaking. For this reason, though I could name numerous truly cutting-edge films on this list, the majority of them are impossible to find. Because of this fact, this list is composed of films that are available and watchable.

Nosferatu (1922)
Casablanca (1942)
Lady in the Lake (1947)
Dark Passage (1948)
Sunset Boulevard (1950)
Strangers on a Train (1951)
Macao (1952)
Seven Samurai (1954)
Touch of Evil (1958)
The World of Suzie Wong (1960)
A Fistful of Dollars (1964)
Robinson Crusoe on Mars (1964)
Grand Prix (1966)
Bullitt (1968)
Wild in the Streets (1968)
Alice's Restaurant (1969)
Easy Rider (1969)
The Wild Bunch (1969)
Billy Jack (1971)
The Last Picture Show (1971)
Two Lane Blacktop (1971)
Vanishing Point (1971)
Zachariah (1971)
Lone Wolf and Cub: Sword of Vengeance (1972)
Superfly (1972)
The Godfather (1972)
5 Fingers of Death (1972)
Enter the Dragon (1973)
Pat Garrett and Billy the Kid (1973)
The Exorcist (1973)
Master of the Flying Guillotine (1975)
Saturday Night Fever (1977)

Star Wars Trilogy (1977)
Apocalypse Now (1979)
Saint Jack (1979)
The Warriors (1979)
My Dinner with Andre (1981)
Tales of Ordinary Madness (1981)
Blade Runner (1982)
Die Hard (1988)
84 Charlie Mopic (1989)
The Killer (1989)
Hard Boiled (1992)
The Player (1992)
Natural Born Killers (1994)
Pulp Fiction (1994)
Casino (1995)
Last Man Standing (1996)
The Blair Witch Project (1999)
Bangkok Dangerous (2001)
Gerry (2002)
The Bourne Identity (2002)

SECTION VI
Asked and Answered

Inside Zen Filmmaking

How should one approach watching a Zen movie?

That's a good question. Let me try to give you a good answer. I think that you need to go into a Zen Film as if you're going into an art museum. You have to see it for what it is. Like I always say, *"You may hate the art of Picasso, but you can't say it isn't art."* You need to go into a Zen Film with that state of mind – that it's art and you may love it or you may hate it, but it's made purely from the sense of art.

I have watched I think about seven Zen Films now. I said to my partner, 'I don't know what these things are, but I'm pretty sure you can project them on the wall and you can walk in and out of them like an installation.' Is that how you feel about them?

Yes, that's basically what it's all about. It's like when some filmmakers have millions-and-millions of dollars, but they still make a bad movie... You know what I mean? So, it's not based upon the amount of money that was spent to make a movie, it's based upon the amount of art that is created within it. That's my entire focus. Making a film that is filled with art. You can start or leave it at any point. Wherever you find yourself within it, that is where you are.

How many people see your movies, as they are not widely available?

In certain geographical locations they've done fairly well. For example, the movie I made with Don, *Guns of El Chupacabra*, did fairly well in Mexico, Central, and South America. A film like

Samurai Vampire Biker's from Hell, (one of my early films), did fairly well in Asia. I think that each film is kind of different. I mean, some have gotten out there more than others. The fact is, if one person sees them that's great and if a million people see them that's also great. I don't think that the size of the audience defines what they are.

How do you fund your films? I mean, I know they don't cost you a lot, but they must take a little bit of money and a little bit of time?

The ideology of *Zen Filmmaking* came out of a kind of group thought between Don Jackson and myself. But, Don was a very different person than me. He would go out and find financiers. He would go out and find funding for the movies we made. From this, in some cases, we had a lot of money to work with. But me, all I saw from that was just the pure nightmare when people would give you money and then they'd expected a sizeable return—which is very seldom the case. Plus, they all wanted to put in their two cents about the cast and/or the story. You mentioned in your email that you had seen *Roller Blade Seven* and *Return of the Roller Blade Seven*. I mean those two films were funded by a person, not a company, and it just became very nightmarish regarding the stipulations that they put on us. So, the films I did with Don are very different than the films I've done by myself. My films; I completely fund myself, out of my own pocket, because I don't want to have anybody's input. And yeah, I've put a lot of my own money into my movies. But, that's okay. I'm not doing it to make money. I'm doing it for the art of cinema. If they make money; that's great. If not, that okay too.

How do you finance your films?

Basically, as you know, I'm an author and that's probably where the majority of my film budgets comes from. Like yourself, I'm also a journalist, and that's also how I make money. And, I do make money from the sales of my movies. I'm also hired to direct music videos quite frequently; especially for the Japan market. Plus, I make some money as an actor and stuff like that. From all of those sources, that's how I finance my films and my life and lifestyle.

How much money does it cost to make your movies? For example, how much money did Vampire Boulevard cost?

Vampire Boulevard that was pretty low key. I think that was around $300.00 US; maybe just a little bit less. Movies like *Undercover X* and *Hitman City,* which I filmed both here in the States and in Asia—those cost a little bit more money due to travel expenses. *Undercover X* was shot in Seoul and Tokyo. *Hitman City* was filmed in Hong Kong and Macau. I mean, the travel expenses alone cost money, so it is hard to calculate the film's actual budget when you take those factors into consideration. Plus, as I only fly First-Class and I only stay in 5-Star hotels, it can get kinda pricey. (Laughter).

Do you have that wide of a following of martial artists? I mean, I see that some of your films, particularly the ones you made with Donald G.

Jackson, cost a lot of money to make; upwards of a million dollars. That's a lot of money to spend on a movie where you won't necessarily make that all back.

Well... I don't know if it is the people that know me as a martial artist who are actually the ones seeing my films. That being said, all of my books are published through major publishing companies, and I've been involved in the martial arts since I was six years old. And, I started writing on the subject maybe twenty years ago or so. Plus, I write a lot for the martial art journals. From this, my name and face are out there a lot and my books on the martial arts sell pretty well. And, as you probably know, I've also written a lot of books about Zen, Zen Buddhism, Yoga, and things along those lines. Those books actually sell even better than my martial art books. So, people do get to know me through those venues. But, to answer your question, yes, I do have a certain following. But, the fact of the matter is, money has never been my focus; art is. Whatever it costs to make the art is whatever it costs to make the art. High budget or low budget, I never think in those terms. Getting a big return on the money that I've spent to make a film never enters my mind.

How seriously should people take your movies?

I mean, that's a hard question... As you mentioned, *The Roller Blade Seven* has been called the worst movie ever made, but to me, that's a compliment because we did not set out to make *Gone with the Wind*. What we set out to do was to make a Zen Film. It was a very conscious movie to make, just as was *Return of the Roller Blade*

Seven. What we did in those two films was very conscious and I think that's what most people misunderstand. What we're doing is what we're doing. It's, for a lack of a better term, *"In your face cinematic art."* You may love it, or you may hate it. Either way is fine. If you call it the worst movie in the world, *"Thank you,"* it's a compliment because at least you're taking the time to watch it and see it because it's not intended to be good or to be bad. It's intended to be art.

I'm still trying to decide Scott... I have to say last night my girlfriend asked me how's it going. I said, this guy is warping my brain. (Laughter). I watched five of your movies in a row. I literally watched 400 bad movies this year. I watched all of them: Andy Miller, Larry Buchanan, Al Addison, and I think you might have broken me (laughter).

Thank you. That's a compliment. I'm glad. I take that as a compliment!

Tell me about some of the motifs that runs through all of the films of yours, Donald's, and your and Donald's together. The smiley faces, what are they about?

Don, god rest his soul... You know, he died a few years ago. He was a little bit older than me and he came out of that whole late 1960s -1970s era where, at least here in America, those smiley faces were everywhere. As a teenager I used to see them and I really hated them. I thought, *"Oh, my God, these smiley faces are everywhere!"* But, to him, being a bit older, he saw them in a different light. It was kind of like some sort of statement on society. And so, when we would make a movie and

205

he wanted to put one in, I began to embrace them, as well. I mean, they are so ridiculous! Now, to me, they're just kind of like a statement on culture and society where smiley faces are in your face for no reason.

What about the blade? The skates and the blade?
That's kind of both a long and a short story. To explain, Don came to me before we made *Roller Blade Seven* as we had tried to make a Roller Blade movie before that but the funding got pulled. So, I went off and did some other stuff and he went off and did another film. But, to answer, the ideology of the skates came out of the whole 1970s era. For example, when he made his first *Roller Blade* movie, that was actually before the inline skates or the term, *"Roller Blade,"* were even invented. Just like the smiley faces, the skates were Don's homage to the *Roller Boogie Era* and everything that was going on in the 1970s. Now, when we started to make *The Roller Blade Seven,* he initially came to me and said he really wanted to take filmmaking to the next level. He asked, what did I think we should do? And I said, *"Well, first of all let's reference the whole samurai thing,"* because Don and I were both really influenced by the Japanese samurai movies, Kurosawa, Sergio Leoni, and people like that. I said, *"Why don't we take this to the next level and let's make the Magnificent Seven. Let's make the Seven Samurai. Let's take your Roller Blade idea and make, The Roller Blade Seven."* So, that's when I actually came up with the concept. Now, you've seen the movie and there isn't really a crew of seven people in the film. There's not just seven

people, there's a lot of people in the movie. But, what there isn't is *The Magnificent Seven,* there isn't *The Seven Samurai.* What happened is, when we actually started out filming the movie, there was. But, we just had so many problems on that movie between our executive producer and what was going on with the original cast and the crew that we actually eliminated most of the people that were going to be central characters in the movie because they were either just too hard to deal with or they couldn't pull off their role. So then, we questioned how are we going to justify the title, *The Roller Blade Seven?* As you just watched *Return of the Roller Blade Seven,* you know how we solved that issue. In that movie, Don's character says, *"The Roller Blade Seven is the highest level of consciousness."* So that's how we justified it. So, the fact is, the film started out totally differently then it ended up. And that's the great thing about *Zen Filmmaking,* a film can start off as one thing and end up as another.

The topless girls? Are they primarily in there because they look good?

Yeah, don't you love beautiful women? Don't we all? That's basically what we were doing. I think it was Roger Corman who said, *"Nudity is the cheapest special effect."* We borrowed from that and put a little bit of nudity into the film.

Do you think everybody is now going to grab a camera and start shooting and calling it Zen Filmmaking?

207

Well, I don't know about that? But, it's fine with me if they do. My personal belief is that most indie filmmakers take themselves way too seriously. You know, it's like most indie people, if you criticize their movie... If they put it on YouTube and somebody criticizes it, or if it's out there and if somebody's writing about it on imdb.com, they get so insulted. I think they just take their projects just way too seriously. A low budget or no budget movie cannot compete with a high budget film. And, that's one of the things I say about Hollywood, *"Everybody is so quick to criticize."* It's really easy to criticize even the greatest movies ever made. You can find flaws in those films if you're looking. I actually don't believe that most people could be *Zen Filmmakers* because most of them take their project, and their whole concept of filmmaking very-very seriously and they work out everything out from A to Z. Whereas in *Zen Filmmaking* it just kind of happens. You just let it happen.

And how do you rate yourself as an actor?

You know, I've never trained as an actor. I don't rate myself as an actor at all. Why am I in all of my movies? (Well, not in all of them, but most of them)? Because, I know I'm going to show up. (Laughter). No seriously. I don't rate myself as an actor at all. What I do know is that I'm going to be on the set at the time the movie's supposed to be shot, which is something you can't rely upon with newbie actor, highly trained, or very famous actors. A lot of times they have their problems or head-trips and don't show up. Me, I'll be there!

What does your family think about your movies?

I don't know if they'll even watch them. I don't know... When my wife watches one she goes, *"Oh God, you're kissing another girl?"* Or something like that. (Laughter). But, you know, it's one of those things, I don't force my movies on anybody. If someone wants to sit around and watch them, god bless them. If not, that's cool too.

Has your wife been in any of them?

Yeah, my wife has actually helped me with a lot of them over the years. I don't know which of my movies you've seen but in recent years there's an Asian girl who kind of reappears, Hae Won Shin. What she's great for is once I get done filming a movie, whenever the story doesn't make any sense, what I do is bring her in and kind of plug her into the movie to give the story justification for people who want things like that; a story. But she hates it.

Thanks for this, but before you go, I'm going to try and get through another one: Ying Yang Insane, Killer Dead or Alive, and Witch's Brew; which is the best and which is the worst of those?

Well, *Ying Yang Insane* was a movie that Don and I did with Robert Z'Dar. You know, the big jawed guy. He is only person in the entire movie. It's really interesting. So, that's an interesting piece of Zen. *Killer Dead or Alive,* is actually a very interesting movie. And what was the other one you said?

Witch's Brew.
    Witch's Brew. That's actually a really interesting movie. Don and I started doing that just before he died. He passed away and then I came in and finished it. But, flip a coin. If you want the most interesting storyline, *Killer Dead or Alive* is pretty interesting.

You sound like a pretty happy dude.
    Oh yeah, life is interesting.

Good luck, Scott. Thank you very much for taking the time to talk to me.
Okay, it's no problem at all.

Speaking with the Zen Film Master

Scott Shaw has spent the past twenty years making some of the wildest no-budget independent films that the world has never seen. With titles such as *Samurai Vampire Bikers from Hell, Max Hell Frog Warrior, Super Hero Central, Vampire Blvd.,* and *Count Vlogula,* to name just a few, Scott Shaw has etched a niche for himself as one of the most eccentric filmmakers in the industry.

Hailing from Hollywood, California, Shaw is much more than just an independent filmmaker. He is also a respected martial artist who has written an enormous number of articles and books on the subject as well as being an accomplished musician and photographer. When he is not making movies, he teaches courses on filmmaking at colleges and universities.

Whereas many independent filmmakers try to climb the Hollywood ladder, Shaw has turned his back on the traditional film industry and focused his career upon his self-developed philosophy of *Zen Filmmaking.* What is *Zen Filmmaking?* I will let Scott Shaw explain that in his own words.

Before we begin, I want to tell you that I have been a fan of your work for some time and I believe I have seen all of your films.

Thank you. Which one is your favorite?

Undercover X.

That's one of my favorites too.

I also really like the editing in Killer: Dead or Alive.
Yeah, that's a fun one as well. Which of my films do you like the least?

I don't want to answer that. Aren't I the one who is supposed to be asking the questions?
(Laughter) Sorry. Ask away.

I know in the past you said that while growing up you saw the downside of the film industry and that is what kept you from becoming involved in it until much later in your life. Being from an industry family myself, I too have seen that side of it. Have you been able to stay away from the turmoil?
For the most part, yes. I really do not run in those circles and I do not go around asking people for money to finance my films like a lot of indie filmmakers do. So I am able to stay pretty clear of all of the nonsense and the melodrama.

As a filmmaker how would you define the kind of films you make?
Zen Films.

Yes, I know that, but your films have a very unique characteristic. Can you explain that?
That's just it. They're Zen Films. There is no definition for a Zen Film. What they are is what they are. Each one is whole and complete onto itself. Each one is different. There is no formula. There is no dogma. There are no requirements. You just go out there and do it and that is what you do.

Do most people understand your Zen Filmmaking

style?

You know, ever since Don Jackson and I made the first Zen Film, The Roller Blade Seven, we knew that people who had an eye for the cinematically abstract and who really studied the intricacies of what we were doing would understand and like it and the people who expected to see a traditional mainstream film, would not. To answer your question, it is 50/50.

Now that you brought up Donald G. Jackson how did you two function as a filmmaking team?

As artists, Don and I had a very similar mind. He, like I, appreciated the bizarre and the abstract. As people, we had very different personalities. He was very explosive. He liked to yell and scream at people and mess with their heads. Me, I am the total opposite. I'm all about making people comfortable and making the world a calmer and peaceful place.

Then how did you work together?

When we worked together, we were of one mind. We never questioned the other's insights. Whichever one of us had the inspiration, the other one just flowed along.

In the past you have stated that Donald G. Jackson used a script for all of the films he created when you were not involved in the project. Is that true? Isn't that against the primary premise of Zen Filmmaking?

Yes, for the most part that is true. But Don was a very spontaneous guy, if someone wanted to go in a different direction, he never forced them to speak only the lines written in the script.

But you just expressed a really big point that many people misunderstand. Everybody seems to think that *Zen Filmmaking* is simply based on the premise of not using a script. That's totally wrong. The use of no screenplay in the filmmaking process is simply a tool to open up the filmmaker's mind to allow spontaneity to be the primary guiding force in a film's creation. By allowing artistic freedom to guide you in the filmmaking process you allow magic, and by magic I mean you allow and accept magical things to happen that you would or could never expect.

So far you've written two books on filmmaking, Zen Filmmaking *and* Independent Filmmaking: Secrets of the Craft. *What are the differences between the two books and what information do they provide?*

You know, I've been making films for a long time now and not only have I been teaching classes and seminars on the subject for years upon years but I receive a lot of questions about filmmaking all the time. What I realized a long time ago is that everybody has the same questions and everybody, including myself, runs into the same problems. The two books spell all of the problems that I have run into and the problems that other indie filmmakers have run into and then the books provide answers and ways to avoid these problems as much as possible. The difference between the two books is that *Zen Filmmaking* is more of an illustration of my personal filmmaking journey in association with a lot of how-to. Independent Filmmaking is more of an overall nuts and bolts discussion and how-to for the independent film industry.

Having seen most of your films I realize that you are constantly changing as a filmmaker from how you tell a story onto editing and all the various visuals. How and why has your filmmaking evolved?

The main component is that technology is constantly making things easier. I couldn't do, or maybe better put, I couldn't afford to do a lot of things, particularly in editing, that I wanted to do in years gone past. Now it's all on your PC. You can do pretty much anything. From that I have been allowed to continually expand and push the barriers within my visions for artistic filmmaking.

You say there are no mistakes in filmmaking. What does that mean?

Most people who want to make a film have the hope and the desire that their film, made with no money, will come out looking like a hundred-million-dollar feature. Moreover, the people who view independent, low and no budget features expect them to look like they had a hundred-million-dollar budget. That is just not the reality of making an indie film, especially when you have limited financial resources. What I mean by there are no mistakes is that you have to enter the process with the understanding that your film is going to turn out the way your film is going to turn out. That is not to say that you don't try to make it look good. But you have to accept your limitations. And the viewers should also be of that same mindset if they are planning to watch a film of this genre. By entering the filmmaking process with this mindset, the freedom of Zen is experienced.

For this part of the interview I would like to speak to you about some of the practical aspects of Zen Filmmaking and how you make your Zen Films.
　Let's do it.

Why no script?
　Like I have discussed for many years, when someone writes a screenplay, they believe they have a great idea. And, maybe they do. When they move forward to creating their film, they believe it will be filmed with precise camera techniques, in perfect locations, with excellent actors portraying the characters. The fact of the matter is, unless you have a lot of money, which most new filmmakers do not possess, that is just not going to happen. Things are not going to turn out perfectly. This is one of the main reasons that many new filmmakers throw in towel and do not complete their films—because they cannot equal what's in their mind's eyes. But, if you take away the obstacle of a script and remove what is supposed to happen, you become free, you are not forcing yourself to equal what you have conceived in your mind. If a filmmaker operates at this level, there is a much greater chance that the film will be completed.

Without a script, how do you get your stories told?
　For each person it is a little different. What I do is to start out with a story idea. Then I get my cast together and have a few places in mind that I plan to shoot. For each day I construct a shot list

that will explain the characters and the story, and then I go out there and do it.

So you guide your actors on the set?

Exactly. But they are not going out there blind. Before we ever begin to film I discus each character with each actor, so they know what they are going to portray and how they are going to achieve that portrayal. If we have the time, I allow actors to meet the other actors in the film. Then when we get on the set, I tell them the basics of the information that they need to discuss for a particular scene, and I let them have at it. This keeps the performances very natural.

You generally work with unknown actors. Why is that?

Hollywood is an impossible game to win. Yet tons of people come here all the time hoping to be stars. The reason I invite new people to be in my films is I want to offer them the opportunity to actually get in front of the camera and get their feet wet. What I am providing them with is a stepping-stone. They are going to be in a film that will be completed. If they never do anything else in the film industry at least they can say I was in that film. But some of them have actually gone on to become very successful actors and actresses.

What is the average budget for your films?

I try to stay right around $300.00.

$300.00! I have seen your films. You mean to tell me films like Hitman City and Vampire Noir only cost $300.00 to make?

Yup.

How do you do that?

Well, first of all you have to know what you're doing. Then you have to have the right equipment and know how to use it. Like I tell my students, if you can't make a movie using only natural light then you have no business being in the film industry.

How does someone learn how to use equipment and make quality films like you have with such a low amount of money?

It is all about practice and getting out there and doing it.

So you suggest people practice making films?

Absolutely. You don't have to go out there and make a feature film your first time out like I did. Just get out there with a camera every day and make film shorts or just practice with it seeing how it captures images and how it reacts to light. From this, when you actually get ready to make a film you will have the techniques in place to do it right.

What kind of equipment do you use?

That really depends on what I'm doing. Over the years I have used pretty much every camera and every format ever created. I own a lot of equipment. Which is one of the ways I can keep my production costs down. But I always like to tell people; you can even shoot movies with your phone. I mean phones shoot 1080 HD, which has a much better image quality than Super 8 and even some 16mm cameras. If the phones had a mic input, because they have pretty lousy audio, you could shoot a whole movie on your phone. I imagine someday some phone company will add a mic jack and then there will never be a need for full-on cameras anymore.

Have you ever used your phone to shoot a scene that made it into one of your films?

Of course. Like most people I always have my phone with me, and I have used it several times to capture footage. But personally, what I do is I always carry a small Nikon or Canon with me. Then not only can I take a photograph if I see something, but I can also shoot high quality footage for my films if an interesting situation presents itself.

You are against getting film permits. Is that true?

It's not that I am against film permits. It is simply that most indie film people do not have the money to rent a location and pay for film permits. The other problem is, once you lock into a single location then your options are severely limited. You have to stay there and that really holds back spontaneous creativity.

The fact is some people believe that it is illegal to shoot a movie without a permit. That is not true. If it is a public place, you have just as much right to be there, doing whatever you want to do, as anyone else. You can't go in there with a Panavision camera, 10-K's and a big crew, but if you stay low key, you are usually fine.

Have you ever been asked to leave a location you were filming at?

A couple of times, but it's rare.

What do you do then?

Just go and shoot somewhere else.

In your films you've shot in places like Tokyo, Taipei and Hong Kong. Why do you film there?

Interesting locations are one of the number one things you need to add to your film if you want to make it look big and give it depth. Whether you film in your community or whatever, the more interesting your locations the better your film with look.

As I spend a lot of time in Asia, I add those locations into my films whenever I can. Tokyo is great. It is a very visually spectacular place and nobody cares if you film there. You can film anywhere and nobody even takes notice. Everybody from the Beasty Boys to Katy Perry have filmed in Tokyo just by showing up and doing it.

How do you respond to film critics? Which is something that each filmmaker must be prepared for.

I don't. I don't care what any negative person thinks. First, let them make a movie and then we'll talk about it.

The fact is, the minute you get into any of the arts you are going to have your critics. That's just the way it is. The sad thing is, their voices always seem to be the loudest. It would be great if the people who had positive things to say would be more vocal, but it doesn't seem like that is going to happen. Positive people always seem to be the quiet ones.

Why do you think some people are so critical?
I don't know. There's a lot of reasons, I guess. Some people want to make a name for themselves and critiquing and criticizing the work of someone else is an easy way to do it. Some people may not like a person or what they stand for and that is their reason. The one thing I do know is that negativity only equals negativity and that is never a good thing.

Do you ever think you will return to acting on the A-level or directing a big film?
Well Cameron, Spielberg, Tarantino or Rodriguez aren't knocking down my door. And Weinstein or Lionsgate isn't ringing the phone of my agent off the hook. So I don't know? But that is really not important to me. I think I have made a niche for myself in the film industry, doing what I do. I make films for the love of the craft. And the reason I teach filmmaking and talk to people like you is that I want to help other filmmakers get out there and live their dreams of making a film. That's the whole basis of *Zen Filmmaking* and that's why I have continued to keep my focus on it. In simple terms, *Zen Filmmaking* removes a lot of the obstacles from the filmmaking process so that films will get completed and filmmakers will get their films made.

Remember the main mantra of *Zen Filmmaking,* "Fun is what it's all about."

In this part of the interview, I want to peer into Scott Shaw the filmmaker and ask you why you do what you do.

That's scary. But let's go.

One of the main things I have noticed about your films is that there is always movement. The character you play, or your other actors portray are either riding on a motorcycle, driving in a car, riding on a ferry in Hong Kong, on a subway in Tokyo or on a ship in Canada. If you or your actors are not on some vessel, then the characters are frequently seen walking or running. In fact, one of your recent films I saw, The Drive, revolves around a constant state of movement. Why is that?

First of all, thank you for realizing this, most people don't.

You're welcome.

At its root, the simple answer is, all of life is about movement. That movement may be small or it may be large, but it is constant. Everything in this universe is in a continual state of flux. I want my films to represent that understanding on a subtle, subliminal level. That is why I always have movement in my films. From a less philosophic aspect, movement adds a great level of visual stimuli for the audience. It draws them it. For example, on a subtle level the audience begins to study what is going on outside the windows of a car as the character drives it down the street. Life and the world we live in is very unique. It is a work of art. I like to bring that art into my films as much as possible.

I understand that you shoot your films wherever your inspiration guides you. Yet where you shoot your films and the sets you use have a very common theme, namely the old or the dilapidated. Why is that?

I'm a city kid. I grew up on the wrong side of the tracks in L.A. In terms of the cityscapes I use, I have forever been drawn to the rundown parts of the city. There is simply something very artistic and beautiful about structures that are in decay and an area that is in its latter stages of existence. In terms of my internal sets, my inspiration is the same. But, they are more of a creation than where I film outside. A good example is; I was watching an old episode of the TV series Adam-12 the other day. Malloy and Reed were supposed to be at three different apartments in a rundown building. But all the production team did was to shift the camera to the other side of the hall. In each scene you could see the same spots on the walls and the team entering the same apartment, but they were supposed to be three different apartments on three different floors. I love the cinematic ridiculousness of stuff like that. So, I embrace it. I recreate it.

You have said that there are hidden elements in all of your films. Is that an example?

Yes. But it is more than simply the sets and how they are used. Like you realized about the movement in my films, the items I place for the camera to see: the things on the walls, the floors, and in the distance are all very revealing. There are hidden objects in all of my films and abstract expressions in the dialogue. It is the viewer that must find them and decide what they mean.

Why do you do that?

That is one of the things that makes watching a Zen Film so interesting. Once you understand this, figuring out the underlying meaning of the locations, the dialogue and the scenes become part of the whole process of watching the film.

In terms of your editing style, you have always used exaggerated edits. Why?

Some filmmakers believe that they can draw the audience into the film. They think that they can cause the audience to lose themselves in a film. That's just not what I'm about. First of all, I don't believe that you can do that. A movie may emotionally affect you, but you never forget that you are watching a movie. It's not real. So, I don't even try to do that. In fact, I do just the opposite. I want the audience of my films to have a unique experience. Something jarring. Something different. I want them to say, *"Wow, that's a cool edit. How'd he do that?"* Or, *"I didn't expect that. That really changed the mood of everything."* This is also why I either have myself or one of my actors glances directly into the camera during each film. As I am sure you know, this is something that is forbidden in all realms of traditional filmmaking. I do this very subtly. You really need to look for it. This is just a subtle reminder to the audience that they are watching a film, and the film is not real. It's also based in the fact; we're watching you watching us. Look out!

The next question is rhythm. You always have very rhythmic soundtracks. Why is that?

Again, there is the deeper level and there is the more mundane answer to that question. Rhythm is so primal. It is so at the root of humanity. It touches something deeply inside of everyone. I want the audience to feel the movement in my films. So, I use rhythm based soundtracks. The other side of the issue is, I like that style of music.

In the past people always seemed to try to draw parallels between Zen Filmmaking and other forms of nontraditional filmmaking. That seems to have stopped. Why do you think that is?

I think it is due to the amount of product that has been released using this unique brand of filmmaking. New Zen Films are made all the time, not only by me but also by other filmmakers who are employing various aspects of the philosophy. From this, it has carved out its own entity.

When I was in film school some of the instructors discussed Zen Filmmaking. It interested a few people like myself but others said it could never work.

Obviously, those people were wrong. There have been a lot of Zen Films created. That's the thing about school, I know because I have spent many years in colleges and universities, first as a student and then as an instructor. The thing is, students say a lot of things all based on the fact that they believe they are soon to be the master of the universe. They believe that all of their dreams are going to come true. They think that they know everything and whatever they believe is right. This is especially the case in a subject like filmmaking where a few people have become the king of the world. But it is rare. Most people do not become that successful. That's one of the main reasons I created *Zen Filmmaking* and have continued to focus on it. Not only does it remove many of the obstacles from the filmmaking process, but it also allows films to be created that are perfect within their own perfection. They can be whatever they turn out to be. No judgment. That's Zen.

Will you always be a Zen Filmmaker?

I believe that every filmmaker must base the creation of their films upon a philosophy. Mine is obviously the philosophy of *Zen Filmmaking*. If you don't have a philosophy, then your film simply becomes an attempt to mimic what others have done in order to gain fame or financial success. So to answer your question, yes, I will always be a *Zen Filmmaker*.

Recently you've been discussing how Zen Filmmaking has evolved to the non-narrative film. What does that mean?

As I said to you previously, there is no dogma within *Zen Filmmaking*. It is as free and as creative as the filmmaker chooses it to be. For me, I realized that it was time to move away from story structure altogether. As you know, one of the main concepts of *Zen Filmmaking* is that the stories have all been told. So why try to retell a story that has been told a thousand times before? Thus came the non-narrative Zen Film.

What does that mean and how do you create a non-narrative film?

You mentioned you saw the Zen Film, *The Drive*. That is a non-narrative film. To create a non-narrative Zen Film, the inspiration comes from everywhere, anywhere. I don't know? Where does inspiration come from? But how you create a non-narrative Zen Film is that you capture a series of shots and then weave them together to make a cinematic collage of images that draw the viewer into the space of the abstract, into the space of Zen.

Will you ever go back to making a dialogue driven film?

First of all, my films have never been dialogue driven. Yes, there is dialogue, but they are driven by the essence of pure cinema, artistic cinematic images brought together to shape a collective whole. But sure, if and when the inspiration strikes, I will make another film that employees dialogue.

You mention Pure Cinema. Was that an inspiration to you?

Think about this, *Cinéma Pur*, (Pure Cinema), was created by filmmakers like Chomette, Léger, and Clair in the early part of the twentieth century. Filmmaking was new at that point in history and these people were already attempting to step back and make it a more pure and organic process. Those people lived in a different age than we live in. They possessed a different set of available tools and influences, yet they sought to bring filmmaking back to an artistic source-point. Me too. That's what *Zen Filmmaking* is all about. Is *Zen Filmmaking* based on *Pure Cinema?* No. Am I influenced by it? No. But, I do appreciate their ideologies as I have walked a similar path of inspiration.

What made you become an independent filmmaker?
Wow, that is a deep question and there are probably a million answers. Mostly I've always been an artist. Since a very young age I was also a photographer. At a certain point it just becomes a natural progression for me.

Most independent filmmakers seek out production companies to finance their films. Why haven't you followed that path?
Because I don't want anybody controlling what I do. If somebody is paying you then they control what you create. If someone is controlling you, if someone is telling you what you must do and when you should do it, then it is no longer art. I am an artist. You may love my art, you may hate my art, but my films are made with art as their focus. If someone is financing you, they have one goal and that is to make money. To make money you have to supply a product that the masses will appreciate. You've seen my films; do you think the masses can appreciate them?

Yes, I do.
Wow, that's a first. Thanks.

With this I end the interview with Scott Shaw the Zen Filmmaker.

Scott Shaw is a truly unique believer in art and the art of filmmaking. Though his words may have a certain seriousness to them, there was never a moment that he did not possess a big smile on his face. As we parted company he said, "If you ever need any help making a film, don't hesitate to call." I think this is probably the biggest revealer about Scott Shaw. He is a truly helpful individual who does what he does not only to create art as he sees it but also to lend a hand to all of us who are attempting to climb the ladder in the filmmaking industry.

Thank you Scott Shaw.

Scott Shaw Books-in-Print Include:

Apostrophe Zen
About Peace: A 108 Ways to Be At Peace
    When Things Are Out of Control
Advanced Taekwondo
Arc Left from Istanbul
Ballet for a Funeral
Bangkok and the Nights of Drunken Stupor
Bangkok: Beyond the Buddha
Bus Ride(s)
Cairo: Before the Aftermath
Cambodian Refugees in Long Beach, California:
    The Definitive Study
Chi Kung for Beginners
China Deep
Echoes from Hell
Essence: The Zen of Everything
e.q.
Guangzhou: A Photographic Exploration
Hapkido: Articles on Self-Defense: Volume 1
Hapkido: Articles on Self-Defense: Volume 2
Hapkido: Essays on Self-Defense
Hapkido: The Korean Art of Self-Defense
Hong Kong: Out of Focus
Independent Filmmaking: Secrets of the Craft
In the Foreboding Shadows of Holiness
Israel in the Oblique
Junk: The Backstreets of Bangkok
Last Will and Testament According to the
    Divine Rites of the Drug Cocaine
L.A. Street Shots: A Photographic Exploration
L.A.: Tales from the Suburban Side of Hell
Los Angeles Skidrow: 1983
Macau in Black and White

Marguerite Duras and Charles Bukowski:
The Yin and Yang of Modern Erotic Literature
Mastering Health: The A to Z of Chi Kung
Nirvana in a Nutshell
Northern Thailand: Chiang Mai and Beyond
One Word Meditations
On the Hard Edge of Hollywood
Pagan, Burma: Shadows of the Stupa
Roller Blade Seven: A Photographic Exploration
Sake' in a Glass, Sushi with Your Fingers:
Fifteen Minutes in Tokyo
Scream of the Buddha
Scream: Southeast Asia and the Dream
Scribbles on the Restroom Wall
Samurai Zen
Sedona: Realm of the Vortex
Shama Baba
Shanghai Whispers Shanghai Screams
Shattered Thoughts
Singaore: Off Center
South Korea in a Blur
Suicide Slowly
Taekwondo Basics
Ten to Thirty
The Chronicles: Zen Ramblings from the Internet
The Ki Process: Korean Secrets for Cultivating
    Dynamic Energy
The Little Book of Yoga Breathing
The Little Book of Zen Mediation
The Lyrics
The Most Beautiful Woman in Shanghai
The Passionate Kiss of Illusion
The Screenplays
The Tao of Chi
The Tao of Self Defense

The Voodoo Buddha
The Warrior is Silent: Martial Arts
 and the Spiritual Path
Zen Mind Life Thoughts
The Zen of Life, Lies, and Aberrant Reality
The Zen of Modern Life and the Reality of Reality
TKO: Lost Nights in Tokyo
Urban India: Bombay, Delhi, Lucknow
Varanasi and Bodhi Gaya:
 Shade of the Bodhi Tree
Wet Dreams and Placid Silence
Words in the Wind
Yoga: A Spiritual Guidebook
Yosemite: End of the Winter
Zen and Modern Consciousness
Zen Buddhism: The Pathway to Nirvana
Zen Filmmaking
Zen in the Blink of an Eye
Zen Mind Life Thought
Zen O'clock: Time to Be
Zen: Tales from the Journey
Zero One

THE ZEN

www.ingramcontent.com/pod-product-compliance
Lightning Source LLC
Chambersburg PA
CBHW070533170426
43200CB00011B/2410